rants + ramblings

rants + ramblings
Living life with the perspective of death

by Timothy Secord

TATE PUBLISHING *& Enterprises*

Rants and Ramblings
Copyright © 2007 by Timothy Secord. All rights reserved.

This title is also available as a Tate Out Loud product. Visit www.tatepublishing.com for more information.

No part of this publication may be reproduced, stored in a retrieval system or transmitted in any way by any means, electronic, mechanical, photocopy, recording or otherwise without the prior permission of the author except as provided by USA copyright law.

Scripture quotations marked "NIV" are taken from the *Holy Bible, New International Version* ®, Copyright © 1973, 1978, 1984 by International Bible Society. Used by permission of Zondervan Publishing House. All rights reserved.

The opinions expressed by the author are not necessarily those of Tate Publishing, LLC.

Published by Tate Publishing & Enterprises, LLC
127 E. Trade Center Terrace | Mustang, Oklahoma 73064 USA
1.888.361.9473 | www.tatepublishing.com

Tate Publishing is committed to excellence in the publishing industry. The company reflects the philosophy established by the founders, based on Psalm 68:11,
"The Lord gave the word and great was the company of those who published it."

Book design copyright © 2007 by Tate Publishing, LLC. All rights reserved.
Cover design by Leah LeFlore
Interior design by Lindsay B. Behrens

Published in the United States of America

ISBN: 978-1-60247-878-7
1. Christian Living   2. Spiritual Growth/Contemplative Life
07.10.25

Death
>   If Only
>   and other self-discovery
>   into the life I could have lived.

dedicated to

All the special people who kept on believing in me and my ramblings.

And to those who long for more and fight to find it.

contents

foreword 11
preface: my apologies 13
someday 15
potato salad 16
drowning on dry ground 25
awful masterpieces 32
time stood still 36
hindsight 45
tribute 48
change the world yet? 52
crossing cultures 57
choices 61
something/anything 64
a long dark snow storm of the soul 70
obsession, isolation, & rollercoasters 74
thank you 82

mini me	87
the greatest chapter...almost	90
dead grass	104
nothing	109
blinded by sight	112
secrets	114
confessions	119
it's not about me	122
the people in the white houses	126
sh*t, cigarettes, and postmodernism	132
life in eight short chapters	138
i could die tomorrow	156
shoulda, coulda, woulda	161
wholly half	164
i'm not right	168

foreword

Tim had a '79 Buick Regal. And not a particularly nice one, though he would have argued that point at the time. That is, until he blew a head gasket on the way to some cow town in southern Michigan. As it turns out, head gaskets are important, as is the free enterprise system that set the price of such a repair. That is how we found ourselves staring at a lifeless small block V-8 and a Chilton's repair manual in my mother's garage. Tim and I had known each other for a while, and we were friends. But after four days in that garage in the middle of a Michigan winter, we had become more than self-taught mechanics; we were brothers in a life-long quest to change the world.

I tell you this, oddly, because I am not a theologian. Usually people who write forewords for Christian books are theologians, or at least know as much about the subject matter as the author, thereby lending credibility to the work. That is not the case here. I am not an expert on youth ministry. I am not an expert on the post-modern church. I am not an expert on why the Christian culture we have created is so bent on ignoring the tough questions and unlovable people. These are Tim's areas of expertise, and I will defer to him. I suppose I am writing this foreword because I am an expert on Timothy Lee Secord. And if you want to know what is in the heart of a man, walk through 18 years of real life with him and listen to what he says when no one else is listening. When there is no agenda other than finding God buried in the brush pile of our lives, and asking Him to light a fire.

This book is not an act. It is not the result of a survey or a case study. It is not carefully worded to make us feel good about the rut we are in. This book is Tim's heart on paper, and Tim's heart is all about making people uncomfortable the way Jesus did. For years he has been a ticking bomb slowly building in intensity as he has watched church and Christianity and life done wrong by so many. Kids quietly shunned from youth groups for being "worldly." Pastors who are unwilling to lead their congregations out of the dull, crippling monotony of "the way we've always done it." A Christian sub culture collectively asleep at the wheel while hopeless people look to us to step on the gas. Tim finally exploded, thank God, and the debris of hope, forgiveness, and Christ's passion for the broken is strewn urgently amid these pages.

This book is not for the religious. No offense, but if religion is your thing, there is a whole section dedicated to it at Barnes & Noble. This book is about the life we could all be living if we really believed in a radical, controversial, table-turning Jesus- friend to prostitutes, liars, cheaters, and underdogs everywhere- and tried to be just a little more like Him. So take it in, my friend, and prepare to have your engine rebuilt like that old white '79 Buick Regal. Just don't catch fire and burn to the ground like it did.

—Paul Alan, musician
Paulalan.com

preface: my apologies

You never begin a speech with an apology. That is the first thing I remember in speech 101. Someone (we'll call him a friend) got up to give his assigned speech and began with, "I'm sorry this isn't better but I..." and then he listed all the excuses he had for not getting the assignment done.

What are you looking at? It wasn't me. I would never do that. But if it had been me, let me just tell you that the teacher would have jumped all over me and then made me do it over. Two speeches for a lousy C plus. But it wasn't me—really!

The years have passed since I learned that lesson. And in honor of my teacher, I will begin my first book with an apology. I love pay-backs! It's just how my twisted mind works. This is for, um, my friend and those two embarrassing speeches and all the bad grades that I, I mean he didn't deserve—so there.

If what you are about to read seems a little disjunct or disjointed at times, it is by design I assure you. This is a book about life and life is like that. It's not always logical. It doesn't always fit or flow as much as we would like.

It should also be said right up front that this is not my autobiography. It is a book about the life of this animal known as human. Certainly it is taken from several of my experiences but

I hope it connects with yours. I hold that there are common threads and themes to all life. It is these threads that I write about. Think of it as part fact, part fiction and part fantasy. After all, isn't that life?

someday...

I Want...

I Want so much...

I want more than I have. I want to go deeper. I want to live before I die. I want to see with more than my eyes. I want to know more, love more, feel more. I want more.

More...

But I settle. Settle for less. Settle for comfort. Settle for the safety found in the routine. I settle. I wait. I wonder. I want more.

More...

Before it's too late. I want to wake up. I want an adventure. I want romance. I want to look back on my life and smile. Life moves pretty fast. I dream. I plan. I wait and poof! It's over. Just like that. Over.

I want so much more...

What about you? Is, "It won't happen to me" good enough? What do you want? Who are you really? The "you" nobody sees?

It's not too late to change, is it? You're not dead yet, are you? You will be, you know? Dead that is.

You are going to die. It's always sooner than you think.

It Will Happen to You.

potato salad

"That *can't* be good for you." The comment snapped Corey's attention back to the present. Looking down, he saw the half-chewed Styrofoam coffee cup. He realized that he had been nervously biting it to shards. The fragmented pieces had collected around his feet.

"I don't know if I can do this," came his short response. His father looked at him with a mixture of love and pain in his eyes.

"You can. You will. You'll get through it. He would want you to speak."

"I'm not a preacher and I don't do well in front of people; that was *his* thing."

"We don't need a preacher, we've already got several of them upstairs getting ready. We *need* a friend to share his story. Just talk from your heart."

His story, *my* story, for so many years, it was our story. "Where do I start?" Corey wondered, as he anxiously looked around the church as if searching for an answer.

His father walked over to the table and picked up the notes. "Looking for these?"

As he took the pages, he glanced at the first words, "Tim was a lifelong friend, someone who was always there." How do you sum up a lifetime of thoughts in a few words? And why did that lifetime have to be so short? This whole thing sucks. Corey glanced at the clock that hung on the Sunday School wall. Fifteen minutes to go. "Can I have a few minutes alone?" His father gave him a hug.

"I'll see you upstairs," he said, and then he was gone. Corey stood alone with his thoughts. He flashed back to his childhood. He couldn't remember the exact time he met Tim but they were young; just two or three years old. Together, they had seen some great times and survived some difficult ones. A faint smile crossed his face as he remembered how his mother would get so mad when he and Tim would giggle for no apparent reason at the supper table in that old farm house. They had grown up, year after year, as best friends.

As Corey filed through his memories in search of stories to share, he could plainly recall the expression on Tim's face the day they went to get a tractor from the barn.

"He had to move my car and the poor kid backed straight up into the semi," Corey practiced saying aloud. "He was so scared."

The memories rolled on in his head like old home movies. He remembered getting the snowmobile stuck in the ditch; our first dates and the trips to the dances. It all went by so fast. Before I knew it we were out of high school and ready for college. We ran straight into the real world with no fear. "During one of the lowest points in my life," Corey remembered, "Tim drove for hours to my college campus just so I wouldn't have to be alone. And now he's gone."

With time running out on the clock, Corey headed to the sanctuary. Most people were already seated. Up front, on the stage were five chairs. In front of the chairs was the pulpit. In front of the pulpit, the casket. Fragrant flowers everywhere failed miserably to mask the empty ugliness that stifled everyone in the room. Corey could hear sniffles and sobs behind him as people tried to compose themselves before the service started.

Corey choked back the lump in his throat. It was crazy; a senseless accident and then…nothing. Just like that and a life is over. Corey looked back at the casket. "I think I'm going to be sick," he whispered under his breath.

The funeral service began with a hymn and some opening remarks by Pastor Rick. Rick had married Tim and his wife. Pastor Rick shouldn't be here. He shouldn't have to do this. It shouldn't have happened. More songs. A prayer. Corey was lost in thought. He remembered the day Tim decided to go into the ministry. He looked out and saw Tim's father. He had been so proud of his son that day. Tim felt a call to go into youth ministry and never looked back. He enrolled in a Christian college and four years later, had a full-time job at a church in Ohio. Two years after that, he was ordained.

Corey looked up as he heard the pastor say something trite about the 'frailty of life.' *Life,* he thought, *life is so strange.* It can drag on forever when you are waiting for something to happen and then when you look back it was only a blink. How did we go from carefree kids to college students, to jobs, to husbands, to families, to the end? It can't be the end. *How long do I have?* Corey wondered. *There is still so much to do, and so much I should have said to Tim. Now I'll never get the chance.*

Corey's stomach churned. *It's almost my turn. I wonder if anyone can tell how scared I am?* Flipping through his notes one more time, a sentence caught his eye. 'Life is an adventure.' Tim certainly was adventurous. He loved skydiving and parasailing; skiing in Colorado; rock climbing, anything dangerous. Corey looked up. Pastor Nathan was speaking now. As kids, all three of them had been in youth group together. Nathan had gone into the ministry, too. He was sharing about Thrive. A while back, Tim and Nathan had started a leadership camp for high School students. They were tired of the normal, boring Christian youth camp experience, so they came up with Thrive. Each year, students from around the state were selected to be a part of Thrive. They would meet in Michigan, drive to Kentucky for orientation and then head to the wilderness in Tennessee. There they would spend a week bonding, growing and truly living. There was rock climbing and repelling, whitewater rafting, spelunking, overnight hiking, jumping off of rocks into icy water and showering under waterfalls. The students practiced leadership skills and grew spiritually. But mostly, Tim wanted to make sure that they learned how to live life to its fullest while they were still young people. As Corey looked out into the pews, most of the Thrive community had shown up.

Nathan finished and sat down. Tim's friend Paul began to sing a song. Corey was next. No one had talked about the six years Tim served as a firefighter. There had to be some great stories there. He even made the newspaper a few times. He had gone into a couple of bad blazes and come out unscathed. That's the irony of life. So many dangerous choices, but nothing ever happens. It gives the false sense that there is always more time. Why do we always think we have as much time as we'll ever need?

Time to plan; time to do; time to dream and love. *How much have I put off relying on one more tomorrow?* Corey wondered as he looked up. Oh. They were waiting for him. He wiped his nose, stepped to the pulpit, took a deep breath and began.

"Tim was a lifelong friend. Someone who was always there."

And that was that. The funeral concluded, the graveside was over, a life ended. All that was left were the memories and the luncheon back at the church.

Potato Salad

"Pass the potato salad." "Crowd's thinning out." "I'm exhausted." "Nice service." "Beautiful weather."

Beautiful weather? What the heck are you talking about? It's me, Tim. I'm the one whose dead and that's the best you've got? Trivial comments about food and weather? Oh, and *you're tired?* Excuse me. I certainly didn't mean for my demise to tucker you out. Tell you what, sweetheart, I'll trade places with you.

Wouldn't that be nice? Another chance. One more shot; a chance to get it right, now that I know what is at stake. The ultimate "If Only."

That's the last mistake I'll ever make. No really, at least in the earthly world. I don't think you can screw up in the next. If you can, most likely it won't be to this extent. I'm fairly sure there are no second chances at life. So I offer this book. A messy view of life with the hindsight of death.

I could launch into an expose on living and learning from my mistakes. A kind of 'don't-follow-in-my-footsteps' scenario or an 'it's-not-too-late-for-you' plea. It's all bull anyway.

Because *you* are alive and, therefore, won't listen or are unable to hear or something like that. Whatever the reason, I'll save my breath. Let's just call this something I did for myself. Peer over my shoulder if you like, but don't expect any how-to or self-help crap. Take from it what you will. As for me…I'm cold. Apparently it's the kind of cold you don't warm up from. Honestly, I don't see much changing even if I did wake up. That's just not who I am.

Look. Do you see the guy asking for the potato salad? He thought I was a saint. Of course the one *passing* the potato salad remembers me as a jerk. As for the truth, I don't even like potato salad. I don't like being dead either. I'm stoked about this afterlife thing, don't get me wrong. And the IRS can kiss my dead butt 'cause they aren't getting another dime out of me. Death has its moments. No, what I don't like is the fact that I'm not alive. Or rather, that I can't interact with the living. My guess is that while you are reading, you're assuming that *you* are alive. I have my doubts. Nothing personal, but I'm pretty sure that you are just as dead as I am.

I have lived for a long time and was even *alive* part of the time. But, in all that living, I saw very few 'alivers' out there. Most were like me, and yes, like you; content to use up oxygen, to take up space, and to just exist. Most of our lives are just borrowed from someone else anyway. At least in this coffin, there is no more *pretending* to be alive. It's not like I'm going to sit up and say boo! Although that might be cool. Should have done something cool before they shoveled all this dirt on me.

I wonder what they put on my tombstone. "Better luck next time." That would be funny if it wasn't so depressing. Most of us live so casually, like there is a next time; some great cosmic do-over. Humans just don't get it. And the ones that do figure it out never make the six o'clock news. I never made the news. It's not that I want to be remembered that way. I just want to have done something memorable, something for myself that wasn't completely selfish. Do you get it? Of course not. You're living and I'm fertilizing flowers.

It's funny, I never thought about how much birth and death are the same. They should have the same name. Journey, maybe. I journey into this world and journey out into the next and have absolutely no control over either. Just an aside to those of you that think you have control, you don't. Write me off as weak or cynical or whatever the term may be, but you don't have the same view that I do. Talk to me at *your* funeral potluck. I guarantee it will be just the same as mine with different people saying the same trivial pleasantries and clichés. I hope they don't have potato salad at yours.

Hold on, I changed my mind. I don't like the name journey. It conjures up images of seeking and of adventure, of discovery and of struggling to overcome. That is the ideal name, but not at all practical. Most of us don't journey. Oh what the heck, we lie about being alive, let's lie about the name, too. Journey it is. Besides, 'robotic, narcissistic, apathetic drifting' is much too long of a title. What? You don't appreciate my sarcasms and belittling of your existence? Hey, sue me. Wait. Ha! You can't. I'm dead. So if you don't like it, you have two choices:

1. Get up, start truly living life and prove me wrong or
2. Shut up and eat some more potato salad. Do what you will.

I'm out. I'm done. I'm good.

Sinner or Saint. Loved or hated. Ready or not? Unforgiven or covered with grace. Eternal void or eternal rest. I'm there.

Nothingness or completion, whatever this journey holds, I now know. And here's the perpetual kicker, I'm not telling. You've got to figure it out for yourself. No cheating. You can't solve this one with that noodle atop your head. You don't get to see it, hear it, taste it, touch it or sniff it. It's the eternal riddle: How do I discover the infinite with the finite before I become extinct? And I am fairly sure the answer is not in that nasty potato salad you are shoveling in your mouth.

Potato salad...what were they thinking?

In an instant, we can lose it all. We struggle and mêlée just to keep our heads above the water. Our greatest fear is that we lose it all, that we lose control. Reality is that we have no control whatsoever. Control is an illusion. The illusion recycles the fear. Why not lose it all? What do we have worth hanging onto anyway?

drowning on dry ground

So that's it? A life worth of living or pretending to live, ends just like that? A touch anti-climatic I think. There are no famous last words, no heroic feats of daring. I just die alone? This doesn't feel like the movies at all. Like most of my life, that too was a lie. No, not like this! There still has to be time. There still has to be something to say. Something other than I never thought it would happen to me. I have a story to tell and things to set straight. I want to change. I want to live. I can't believe it! So that's it?

I suppose I should start again. Walking in during the final scene of a movie or play just spoils the performance. Too many missing pieces, not enough character development. You don't know whether to love or hate, laugh or cry. Is this a villain or hero? So I will make my way from the opening moments and let you judge for yourself. This is not the great American novel and I suspect that the character is neither a villain nor a hero. In fact, that is my fear; that the character just existed amid millions of others and made no significant imprint on anyone. The character is me. It is my story. I wish I could start again.

The story is mine. Yet if you look closer, dig just a bit deeper, the story is yours. Well not exactly yours to be sure, but it could be yours. Just change a few names and places, swap a sin or two, put in a new addiction or struggle and there you have it…the story of your life. What would it say? If you could write your life story, how would it read? Not just write it as it happened but rewrite it as it could have happened. What then? That is the dream I suppose. Two books: the first, your life exactly as it happened and the second, your life the way you wanted it to happen. The dream that the two books are identical. Word for word they are the same. No regret, nothing to change, you lived life to the fullest, the perfect story.

Is it possible? Does such a life exist? I don't think the perfect life would be perfect. The perfect world would be a perfect bore: Much too predictable. Philosophical thought says that you can't know light without a concept of darkness. Without an understanding of pain there would be no pleasure. I believe this is true. Close your eyes and imagine a perfect life. Everything you ever wanted exactly when you wanted it. No struggles, no problems but no adventure and no excitement. The perfect life would become a TV dinner. It would look great on the cover but would have no taste, no flavor. No the perfect life would not be void of struggle and pain. Perfection would lay in the choices you made in those moments. I don't think you look back on your life and regret the hard times. One may regret how he responded in those hard times. A dear friend and wise sage once told me that nothing grows on the mountain top; it's just rock up there. Sure there is a great view, but the growth takes place in the valley. As I look back on my life, I grew the most in the difficulties, the valley. A life of perfection would be a superficial, meaningless existence. Perfection would become too predictable. God in his infinite wisdom placed us in a world where anything can happen and usually does when you least expect it. It is under these conditions that legends are born.

It's true I wanted to be a legend. I had a dream of standing on stages in front of thousands of people who wanted to hear me! Everyone knew my name. I was a superhero who would never be forgotten. Now, now my life is over and I realize I never took the dream out of my head. I am looking back over a life of should've, could've, and would've. My epitaph will read, "What if?" Now I'm back to the end of the movie again. Forgive me, I have to stop doing that. Funny thing though, I never once in my life said I want to waste my life. Today I want to live a mediocre life and just waste my time. Hey, maybe I will make a few bad choices today and destroy my future. The thought never entered my mind. I guess I just never thought about it at all.

I should have known. I should have been able to see. Status quo super heroes are neither heroic nor super. They are just ordinary. I don't want to be ordinary. I have these dreams in my head, this burning in my heart, but what do I do with it? I don't even know when the dream began. There were defining moments of course. Moments when I caught just a glimpse, a vision if you will, but I never knew what to do with it. The dream was always there but the timing was never right. When I was a child I thought I was just a child. What can a child do? My brothers and sisters taught me that. "You are too little." "This is for big people." "Maybe when you grow up." I guess I'll just have to wait…so I waited. But in high school, I got into friends, sports and cars. Friends take time. Cars break. Looking good in sports takes money.

I got a job. When I get out of high school things will be different, I reasoned with myself. I will be a free man. Parents won't be telling me what to do. I'll have all the free time in the world. Things will be different. I will get my life together then. I will live the dream then. I really want to change the world. I want to make a difference. But I don't know how. Maybe college is the answer. So I graduated from high school and was free. Free to work like a dog to pay for school. Free to spend every waking moment studying things I don't even want to learn. Free to say 'screw it' and run away for a week and blow off some steam; release the pressure. No one ever told me that 'blowing off steam' was so expensive or so addicting. It took its toll in every area of my life. Well, just four years. After that, I would have gotten married and settled down. Couldn't worry about changing the world; I had to live life. I'd never get another chance like this again. I missed this and I would not get a second chance. When I married there would be plenty of time and money to seek this illusive dream. I would have made a difference then. Just you watch. I could have stopped anytime I wanted to. I'd just turn my life around overnight. Four years of doing what I wanted didn't a habit make. No downward spiral here; no problem at all. The problem with hindsight is that by the time you can see clearly, it's too late—or so I thought. I should have known!

So school is out and I was engaged. So in love, she is the one. Nothing would ever change this feeling. I would feel like this forever. Whenever I looked at her, sheer excitement. No really, I was that dumb. I really believed it. Then came the careers and mortgages, and children, and school bills, and schedules, and daycare. Oh, if only I could be fifteen again and be free. Wait. I didn't think I was free back then either. What the heck is going on here? What about the dream? Forget the dream, how did I get this old and this cynical? You know the rest of the story. It is America's story. Work hard to make money, make money to enjoy life, but have no time to enjoy life because you are too busy making money. Why is it so hard to see this trap while you are in it? What could I have done differently? How could have broken the chain?

There it is: the overview to my story, to your story. It seems that the great American dream is a nightmare. We all spend our entire existence just existing. We work so hard to have it all, only to be left with nothing. Wondering what happened, we search desperately to find that one moment when we lost the dream. Only when it's too late do we discover that the dream wasn't lost in a day. It was lost in the seemingly insignificant choices made over the course of a lifetime. "Sorry, honey, I need to work late again." "Just one more…fill in the blank…what can it hurt." "But no one will ever know." The shortcuts and free lunches have landed us a dead end. The words ill spoken, the intentional pain inflected, the mental games we all play lull us into apathy. It is tough to live a dream when society is selling you a piece of the pie. I am so sick of pie. Yet, we go on buying into it. You have to have this gadget to simplify your life. If I did away with all the gadgets, all that would be left are family and friends. Simplicity is a family vacation in the woods with a lake to swim in. Instead, we spend thousands of dollars and drive or fly thousands of miles to go to a theme park to see a man-made replica of something that resembles a woods and a pool that is crowded and has too many chemicals in it. But the old lake isn't prestigious enough. Life, what life?

Remember the first time you jumped into the lake? No life jacket, parents weren't in the water to hold you up. You just learned to swim. The water was cold but you didn't notice because you were too excited. You were swimming for all you were worth because you didn't want to drown. Nowadays we don't jump in; we are thrown in the deep end. It's not exciting, it's not refreshing, it's just cold. It's lonely. You kick and wail just to keep your head above the sea of people. There are millions there just like you but you don't notice them, you can't notice them. You are too preoccupied with your own fears and struggles. It's my story. It's your story. We are all just drowning on dry ground.

Bad poetry is great when it's yours and you own it.
Even better if no one else gets it!

awful masterpieces

Upon A Walk In The Woods

Too many things to say
Too many words to use
Too many games to play
Too many roads to choose
Wanting to rule the world
I failed inside
To find the man behind these eyes
Welcome to reality
Things aren't always what they seem
Upon a walk in the woods

The tighter I hold on
The farther I slip away
Thoughts and dreams race through my mind
Upon a walk in the woods

Looking back at tomorrow
I see pictures of days gone by
Just a memory–frozen in my mind

When will I realize
Futures aren't built on compromise
Can't fight feelings that aren't understood
It's cold here in the woods

The wind goes right through me
To my soul
Pointing out my downfalls
All I want to be is so far from me
Pretenses fall
At the sound of the starter's gun
Swallow your pride
In the struggle for the finish line
I stand confronting myself
Upon a walk in the woods

This is mine—go write your own awful masterpiece.

"Be Ye Warned!
Beyond This Pointe Thar Be Dragons"

Time is fantasy; this world is about time. Creation points to the Creator; the Creator reaches out to His creation. A child feels what an old man understands. Past, present, and future focus in on the moment that…

time stood still
A boy's journey to the cross

"God, I'm so tired I think I'm going to die!" That is all I had to say during the entire Sunday School class. I sat there on the old hand-me-down couch that had been donated to the church and stuffed into the youth room. The faint smell of musty dust stuck in my nostrils. I stared blankly out the window. The view consisted of a brick window well filled with molding leaves and last year's grass clippings. The sun had melted the snow, so all that remained was dirt and disintegrating foliage. The only sound was the teacher rambling on about something…I heard him mention the cross and then I tuned him out.

"Same ol', same ol,'" I whispered to a friend. He snickered and I went back to my trance-like state. I watched the clock flick away minutes with a mechanical rhythm. The teacher's voice became faint and then faded away altogether. I had entered the world of shadows, the world where you are almost asleep, yet still aware of your physical surroundings. All I heard was the hum of the fluorescent lights overhead. They grew louder and louder. My head fell. The teacher's voice snapped back into clear focus with an immediate intensity. It was accompanied by the laughter of others. I was awake. Class was over.

Rising off the couch, I hung out with friends out in the hallway. Together, we did all we could do in a church basement. Mostly, we just talked of other things. A few minutes passed before I slowly made my way up the double flight of stairs toward the sanctuary. Why did I have to get up on a Sunday anyway? Why? Because of my parents, that's why. I can still hear them lecturing me…

"One day you'll be old enough to make up your own mind about church!"

Yeah! Fifteen isn't old enough? Anyway, I believe in God and all. It's just that church is so, well it's just so inconvenient. I mean, it follows Saturday night. Saturday's the best night of the week! And who made the rule that it had to be so damn early? I'll bet there would be a lot more Christians in the world if church was in the afternoon or on a school night or something. Besides, I've heard it all before. All the good reverend wants is money. If he'd let me stay in bed, I'd mail him a check. And what about Sunday School? *No. You didn't just go there!* Is it possible to teach us something we haven't heard a thousand times? And I know this is going out on a limb, but could it be interesting, please? Nah, I'm dreaming. Anyway, it's always the same thing: Jesus loves you. Jesus died for you. Jesus this and Jesus that. I know all of the Bible stories and, quite frankly, they are getting old.

I snapped out of my rebellion, which raged within the confines of my mind, never to be heard by anyone else. My friends and I marched dutifully into the sanctuary. I keep calling them my friends. I *guess* they were. They are the kids you see on Sunday and Sunday only. You exchange greetings in the hallways at school, but it never goes much beyond that. We get each other through church, but there isn't much common ground outside these hallowed walls. This could be a reality TV. show.

I was feeling particularly foul this morning. The weather was fantastic outside. I felt like a little kid forced to take a nap on a beautiful summer day. Winter was finally over and today was suppose to reach the mid to upper sixties, according to the 'religious' radio station my parents tried to brain wash me with every time we'd climb into the Dodge. The sun streamed through the stained glass. *What a deal,* I thought. *If I had to be up this early, at least I could be outside or riding around with my friends or something, anything.* As I rounded the corner that went to the staircase leading to the balcony, I felt a hand grip my shoulder. It was followed by a familiar voice.

"There you are. Come on. Your father is waiting," commanded my mother.

It didn't faze me. I heard it every Sunday. I could have mouthed the words right along with her. What might have been a real shock is if I would have been *allowed* to go where I wanted to go. If they would have let me sit with my peers and sort out my own thoughts. Let me try to separate my beliefs from theirs; if only for one Sunday.

Fourth pew from the front, pulpit side, on the aisle. What a surprise, just like last Sunday, last year, last decade. I glanced around. *What is this, assigned seating? Don't these people ever move?* My father interrupted my thoughts.

"How was Sunday School, son?"

Possible responses flashed through my mind. "Well father, I hated it! I slept through it, so I couldn't honestly say. It was unprecedented, even more boring than the record setting low from last week!" I mustered up all the rebellion I could and opened my mouth.

"It was okay."

I knew better than to bother getting into it with him. I had mastered this game. I had the routine down. Sunday School began at 9:30. Sleep through it, sneaking in smart remarks whenever possible, and if confronted with an actual question, fall back on "God" or "love" or some other universally accepted answer.

Twenty minutes of free time always followed Sunday School. During this time you could do whatever you wanted as long as you avoided the parlor, chapel, or any other parental gathering place. Church began at 11:00 and usually lasted until about quarter after 12:00. There was always time to kill reading the bulletin, or writing notes back and forth to friends, if any were in the area. Drifting off to sleep was a good way to pass the time, as long as the Parental S.W.A.T. Unit didn't catch you. Other favorite time-passers included adding "in bed" to hymn titles, mocking the choir, or responding with the wrong words during the responsive readings. And of course there was the offering. Ah, the offering. This was a great break from the monotony. Watching the vain proudly drop one one hundrenth of what they make in the plate and then act out what a sacrifice they were making for the church. Other cheap entertainment was watching others squirm and sweat as the plate passes. Sometimes they drop in a few quarters to relieve their guilt and cold stares of others. Once in a while, a toddler would even upset the plate. Double bonus Sunday when that happens! Yet without fail, the time always arrives. The longest and most boring stretch begins: The sermon. It is an inescapable prison. Pastor in the front. Ushers cover every escape door, and a congregation of loving prison guards surround the grounds. All you can do is sit and wait.

It is at this point in the ritual that I would always read the bulletin. Turning it over, the front cover struck a chord of horror. Chills covered me. It was the Easter season. They called it Lent or something like that, but I saw past the facade. I knew the score. What it really meant was a *longer service*. I understood all too well that the pastor would once again tell the story of Jesus' death, of the cross, and of the resurrection. I felt drained. I'll never get outta here. The choir sang. I fidgeted. The congregation bellowed hymns and read responsively. I mumbled some notes out of key and smirked as I obnoxiously changed the words of the responsive reading. They passed the offering plate. Even that seemed dull and uneventful. I sank in the pew and contemplated sleep until I caught my father's dissatisfied stare. Too bad. I sat there defiantly.

The sermon was entitled, "Surprised by Pain." It caught my attention, if only for a moment. The scriptures were from the four Gospel accounts of the crucifixion. I sank back into apathy. Then the pastor bombarded me with a horrifying story. I perked up. He spoke of an innocent man so badly beaten that he could not be recognized. I knew he was talking about Jesus. He told about things I had never realized before. Of how cruel the crucifixion thing (death) was back then. Of the sarcastic charge of Pilate that read, "King of the Jews." He spoke of earthquakes and darkness in the middle of the day. The story had my attention, but on and on he went in a monotone, until I grew tired of listening and I finally tuned him out, just like always. Propping my elbows on my knees and resting my head in my hands, I took the reverent posture of one interested in the sermon and began to drift off into the world of shadows again…

Wham! I felt someone smack me. "I'm awake," I said expecting to receive a glare of death from my mother. Instead, I saw nothing. I shook my head, trying to wake up fully. It was pitch black. I heard people all around. I could feel them pressing in, close around me yet, I saw nothing. It was as if I was blind. I stumbled and fought to regain an upright position. Everywhere, people continued to call out to God. There was a horrible smell in the air. I had never smelled anything like it before. It was the stench of panic, refuge, and death. It choked me. I couldn't breathe. I shut my eyes and screamed.

I don't know how long my eyes were shut. I might have passed out. I lost all sense of time. Reality was gone. I thought the earth shook, but I couldn't be sure. Slowly, I opened my eyes. Phew, relief, I saw light. I wasn't blind. The light burned my eyes, and when they finally adjusted, my relief quickly turned to panic. I was scared. I wasn't in church anymore. I didn't know where in the heck I was. A few people stood in the background. Directly in front of me, a man lay in the dirt on a small hill. I noticed no one else. I felt drawn to him. Cautiously, I made my way toward him. As I drew near, he came into full view. His body lay twisted and mangled. Blood was everywhere. I had never seen so much blood. It was nothing like TV. I thought I must be dreaming, but my mind could never have conjured up such a nightmare. His skin was cut, bruised, and covered with welts. Out of his head protruded spiked thorns. Hair was missing. I noticed something sticking out of his side. I looked closer. It was the head of a spear. I turned away. Ran. Stumbled. I think I threw up. I lay there weeping, confused and alone.

"What's happening?" I cried out. Nothing. I returned to the man, fearing the obvious. I looked down at his feet and then his hands. They had holes torn into the flesh. I looked up and for the first time noticed the rough-hewn, blood stained crosses in the background. A man still hung on one, barely alive. I do not understand how or why, but there I stood face to face with Jesus Christ.

The same man I had grown tired of hearing about in church, wherever *church* was. I saw his face. His mouth elongated, lips torn. Flesh missing from his cheek and his nose covered in blood. Then it hit me. Somewhere within my heart, a floodgate broke and years of lost despair poured forth. I saw his eyes. Still open, but glossed over in a deathly stare. I sat there for an eternity staring into his eyes. They held such love and compassion. Yet, never have I seen such pain. I saw all of life in those eyes, innocence and purity and all of hell's fury. It was all contained in the eyes that stared back at me. I turned away. I was deathly afraid. Turning again, I looked back into his eyes. My own reflection stared back at me. In my panic-stricken state, I turned away for the last time. My gaze dropped and I saw my own hands covered in blood, his blood. I had killed him. This immeasurable pain was because of me.

"This is my body, broken for you. Take, eat. This is my blood poured out for you. Take, drink. Do this in remembrance of me." It was the pastor's voice again. I was shaking. A sheer coat of sweat covered my body. My pulse raced as I looked around. It was my own church. People were taking communion. No one was staring at me. No one even noticed me at all. It had all been a dream. I heard the familiar sound of my mother's voice.

"Are you all right?" She continued before I could formulate an answer. "Here take the elements." And almost as an afterthought she added, "Are you sure you are all right, dear? You were in prayer a long time."

The pastor began to close the service. I listened like my life depended on it. "Christ went down that road for you. He died the worst death imaginable to do the will of the Father. Where do you stand today, this very hour? Have you accepted his death? Or was it in vain? It is more than a story, my friends, much more. The Bible is much more than a book. Neither offers an easy road but both offer life. Eternity is set in the hearts of man. On that fateful day in history, God entered time and destroyed death. Have you visited the cross of Christ? God wills that all would be saved. Let us pray."

I didn't wait for a prayer or even an altar call. I rose and walked forward to the altar. A single tear fell off my cheek. I had experienced the power in Christ's death. I wanted to accept it and get on with discovering the power of His resurrection and life. I had heard the stories all before, but I had never even listened. Somehow, if only in my mind, God had touched me. I didn't need an invitation. I didn't need a pastor to save me. I didn't even care what others thought. The cross lay before me and I had been there. Amidst the old routine, I had been joltingly surprised by pain. It was right there all along. I had never bothered to look. I had never even listened.

hindsight

Anyone who has ever spoken the words, "It won't happen to me," died anyway.

Twenty/twenty

"Home is where the _____ is."

I never knew how to finish that cliché. Today so many homes are torn apart by divorce and anger. Where is the heart? I was one of the lucky ones. This family took me in, loved me, modeled heart and taught me how to make a house a home.

tribute

It is January of 1995. I am leading four youth counselors through a training weekend. As part of the training, the counselors share with the group about people who have made a spiritual impact on their lives. Reflection is good for the soul. It builds faith and strengthens relationships. Their homework assignment is to write a letter of thanks to those people. Was there any question that mine would be to the Schaub Family? Not to anyone who knows me. Today, I stand before others as their leader. It hasn't always been that way…

>I remember as if it were yesterday,
>two small boys giggling at the supper table
>until you would send us away. We were young.
>We were wild. It seemed as if trouble was
>the only thing that could catch us;
>It usually did.
>
>Chasing the dog through the fields,
>dirt bikes, snow forts, basketball, and such.
>I was a foreigner to this country life.
>You took me in and loved me as your own.
>This city boy found a brand new home.

Time passed on, as time will do.
As we grew, our worlds grew too.
Cars and girls and activities galore.
You taught us and patiently watched,
as I tested the waters and learned on my own.

Often I failed and fell, stood only to fail again.
But still you were there with love and concern.
"Be careful. Drive carefully—and be home by 10:00."
Rare it was if we made it home by then.
Yet Sunday morning came and we never missed a service.
Each creaking step on the old staircase, I know by heart.
Corey, Tim—Boys, it's time to get up!

You introduced me to your church and your God,
and helped me along as I made them my own.
Words of wisdom, of love and care.
One thing remained; your family was always there.
I wonder how Wayne ever earned a living
with his shop filled with my cars and my curiosity.
What money he did make I'm sure went to Pizza Sam.
Almost every Sunday we were there.
I added up all the totals from those Sunday restaurant bills.
Two thousand eighty dollars and fourteen cents is what I owe,
for the pizza and pop that you never let me buy.
For that, I could possibly repay you and gladly, I would.
But I could never repay you for the life that you lived.

I'm all grown up now with a family of my own.
Much of what I am, I became in your home.
No, I could never repay you, even if I tried.
My thanks and my love I send for my debt.

I remember Wayne's simple words
as I tried to put my 'thanks' into mine.
"You do the same for someone else someday, too."
And that's what I'll do.

Wherever you are, whatever you do, there is someone who helped you get there. There are people who shaped your life and held your hand along the way. Let them know what their love means. Tell them of the impact they had on you. Even if they already realize it, it always feels good to hear it again.

"We are the music makers; we are the dreamers of dreams!"
—Willie Wonka

change the world yet?

I recently underwent corrective surgery for a chronic immaturity syndrome that was plaguing me. I got married. If you ever want to grow up in a hurry, that will do it. The procedure is fairly painless, although the preoperative process is a real killer. But the end result is life changing.

I was reminded of the whole procedure the other day as my wife brought in the mail. Mr. Postman brought me a package that forced me to review the changes I had undergone. It was a cassette tape containing the wedding song written for me and my wife-to-be, penned by one of my closest friends in the world, Paul.

Paul has forced me to get past my simple Christian faith and to engage the Living Lord. I met Paul when I was a freshman in college. I don't remember all of the details of the first encounters, but what grew out of them was a friendship many people search for their entire lives and never find. Paul was a senior in the local small town Christian high school, and I was attending the Christian college just miles away from his house. We passed the carefree days making food runs to the local thirty-nine cent burger joint. We would make fun of the 'stuffed shirts' at the college and get rejected by most of the college women that we asked out. During all of this, we dreamed of something more.

Together, Paul and I discovered gifts. Paul has a tremendous gift for music and I, well I discovered that I had a gift for *talking* about Paul's gift. Unfortunately, what we lacked was a plan. So, I went on with the business of college and Paul graduated from high School and began his own chapter at an engineering school. All Paul had to do was suffer for five years of his life at an institution of higher learning and he would have it made. He would graduate with a job awaiting him, complete with a starting salary of more than I would ever make in the ministry. But there was a yearning for more. Somewhere deep within was a desire, a dream. Paul had a dream of being a musician. I don't know if anything would have become of that dream if two things had not happened. The first was that God started to move in Paul's life and doors opened like we have never seen. It was the unmistakable hand of God in our lives and we had nothing else to do but to walk through. As we did everything we knew how to do, God did the impossible.

The second thing that happened was Mike. He was my college roommate. Mike knew of Paul's dream of becoming a singer, but Mike was a realist. Paul dropped out of college to chase his dream and Mike thought the whole thing to be a bit absurd. One day, Paul and I entered my dorm and there sat Mike. In the most cynical tone he could muster, Mike asked Paul if he had changed the world yet. That was all it took. We never looked back from that point on. Our mission was clear. There was a world to change, and we were going to change it.

I started booking Paul at churches. He would play in front of groups of twenty youth group kids. We would collect love offerings of about fifty bucks and use the money to buy blank tapes. One Saturday morning, we went into our church and made Paul's very first demo recording. The quality was horrendous by any standard but we kept on. We got an apartment together to better plan our attack on the world's evil, and made plans to tour together. I would set up the concert dates, and he would play. Our dream was to eat dinner with Amy Grant and Michael W. Smith, and to be on Letterman.

It has been years since we set out to change the world. Paul is now in Tennessee, and I am in Michigan. I dug out that old demo tape the other day. A smile found my face as I listened to the whole thing, twice. Okay, maybe it wasn't as good as we thought it was back then. I wonder what ol' Mike would say today? Paul and I moved apart and many would say the world is just the same…But is it? Paul quit a so-called 'sure career' in engineering to chase a pipe dream. I am not touring with him, and people are still starving in Africa. As I look at my children, I see a different story. I am changing my world. I grew up in the middle of multiple divorces. My wife is also the survivor of numerous splits and divorces. As we renew our commitment to God and each other, we live out a change in our world and we will model God's family pattern for our children. With God's help, our children's world will be changed as well. I am trying to change the world of the forty students who meet weekly at our youth meetings, as well.

Even though the way Paul and I now go about changing the world has taken us in two different directions, we remain close friends and keep in touch. God still leads our dreams. They may have been redefined, but they remain. Paul never received that engineering degree. He did make a couple of albums with a band and one solo project as well. He even had a couple of number one hits. But now, he is far too busy dreaming of his own family that will start with the unborn child his wife carries. New life, new dreams.

On one hand, there are the realists of the world saying it can't be done. The world is sinful beyond repair. From that viewpoint, they are correct. The world will never be a utopian paradise. But on the other hand, there are the dreamers who pick up a guitar or sit behind a piano and touch people's lives. If Paul touches even one hundred people with his music, how many lives will those one hundred affect? I wonder where the chain-reaction will lead?

Did Paul ever truly make it to the top? Not by the industries' standards. But when he is eighty years old, he can look back on his life and smile. He could have been stuck sitting behind a desk in a white lab coat making model cars out of clay, but instead, he chose to dream, and the world is a better place because of it.

To Paul, I give my support, my love, and I am forever there, right along side of him, chasing my own dreams. I have a dream of reaching young people for Christ and of writing a book that will touch people of all ages.

"Hey Paul, whatcha reading?"

Willie Wonka said it best, "We are the music makers, we are the dreamers of dreams." I'm still waiting for my dinner with our old music heroes, and I have this funny feeling that I will sit at that dinner table one day, and Mike and all the unbelievers will be eating crow.

There is an old saying that states you can never step into the same river twice. Rivers are constantly flowing and changing. So it is with life. There are three things you can always count on to change. They are: perspective, perspective, perspective.

crossing cultures

In 1990, I was a young, nervous Christian attending a small liberal arts college. Life was good, my relationships weren't. I had been engaged only to break it off. I got involved in a few other relationships, only to end them. Without many friends on campus, I decided to date a girl a few hundred miles away. Knowing I needed a change and because I needed a cross-cultural experience to graduate, I signed up for a trip to Israel. I was to spend a month overseas with classmates I barely knew. My journal from the trip will tell the rest of the story…

I left this country afraid of going, afraid of learning, afraid of trying, afraid of failing, afraid of people, afraid of changes, and afraid of staying the same. I came back not quite so afraid of being afraid…

January 23, 1990…

It has been less than a month since a nervous, borderline Christian boarded a 747 and left America behind in a jet stream. I wasn't sure what I would find or learn overseas: I was just glad to be going. I needed a change in my life…

I barely remember the day I left the land of the free. It seems so long ago. I have done so much since then and changed in so many ways. Now the question looms: Can I live out those changes in America? Somewhere amongst all the rocks (of Israel) I heard the voice of God...

My last journal entry, written during a delay in our departure from Chicago reflects the mood of my entire trip:

"Life was different at 39,000 feet and 600 MPH. One can just start to touch God's awesomeness and beauty; can just start to realize the power of God as a grain of sand starts to realize a beach. It's so peaceful up there. But here I sit on mother earth, still waiting, wondering and doing my best to be patient..."

"I am from the United States of America. The problem is that everyone in Israel knew it. They pegged me as a rich American from a mile away. I never thought of myself as being rich. To me, rich is winning the lotto and never working again, but here, rich takes on an entirely different meaning. Any American in Israel is automatically rich. Yet I am still classifying myself as poor. I have everything and think I have nothing..."

After days of a strict diet consisting of bread and water and Israeli vegetables, how dare you say "Pizza"? Yet Murphy promised to take me out for pizza. Murphy, a Palestinian shopkeeper, is one of the few people I trusted in Jerusalem. We found it, pizza and a place with American music. Murphy, I think I love you. After transcending the small talk and struggling through the language barrier, slowly walls came down. We were no longer two people coming together but were two countries coming together. We represented two different worlds with two different views. As I walked back to the institute I couldn't help but think, I have just had my cross cultural study. If the minds of two people with two different cultures can come together, maybe there is hope...

There were others too, like Julian, a drifter from New Zealand, whom I met while walking through the old city. At the institute, I ate with half a dozen students from African nations and with Oliver from Switzerland. I talked with Paul from Austria, with Koreans and Japanese, with an energetic Annabelle from Mexico City, not to mention my fellow college students...

The plane ride back home was a blur. I was lost in foggy cloud of thought. The past month, which seemed to drag on forever, now seemed like a split second, a mere flash in time. I had experienced a different culture. I learned about the Bible, about Israel, about myself. Earlier I had prayed, "I don't have a fear of flying home, but of landing. A fear of getting home and forgetting." Suddenly, I wasn't so afraid of landing. As I emerged from the boarding tunnel into the bright light of Detroit's Metro Airport, it was a brand new day, a brand new me.

As I close my journal from the trip, I reflect back. I now know that like it or not, there is a great big world out there. We Americans don't have all the answers, and we don't always do everything the best. We can learn from other people and other cultures. Plan a trip and take some time to talk to others who are different than you. Open your mind and take a risk. Can't afford it you say? I couldn't either. However, looking back, now I realized that I couldn't afford not to!

choices

I was told to make them wisely, as if I were in control. As if I were the one making choices…turns out they were making me.

Throughout our mundane routine, there are moments that make the routine bearable. Moments that make...

something/anything

I had a real adult conversation the other day. It has been a long time. If you are married and both working, you understand exactly what I am talking about. A real conversation, a refreshing break from the pseudo conversations that fill our everyday existence. It was a wonderful break from the normal small talk and jokes that normally fill the air. Not that there is anything wrong with talk of the weather and vacations, of children and schools. But sometimes we need to go deeper. We need to touch on a more intimate level: To think, to challenge our beliefs and ourselves.

It is much like the Hollywood experience. You know, the movies you spend nine bucks on and then wonder why you did. And that's just the price of admission. If you want the bag of artery hardening popcorn and two cokes, you will need to take out a second mortgage, and for what? An hour and a half of trivial garbage? TV on a larger screen? Action? Let me guess. The good guy will kill all the bad guys even though he is out manned, out gunned, and they just dropped a bomb on him. Romance? Hmmm…the prince will fall in love, suddenly turn into a jerk, and lose the fair lady. But get this, the fair lady will wait. She will put up with it and still be there when he returns.

No matter what comes their way, they will live happily ever after or at least end up in bed together. And comedy? I'm not even going to go there. Let's just say they're so 'funny' that you can't take your children to most of them.

So why do we do it? Why do we keep coming back for more? (Aside from the fact that romance, sex, action, and violence are addicting.) Well, if you are anything like me, it is because you've seen *Schindler's List* or *The Color Purple*. It is because scattered between the boring, trashy, and ridiculously stupid flicks, you were there when *The Passion of the Christ* opened and you are a better person because of it. It is because you went into a theater and saw a classic in the making. You witnessed the triumph and tragedy of the human spirit on the screen and it touched you. It took you deeper, and made you think. It challenged you and your belief system. You left in silence with a tissue in your hand, and you left changed. Those are the movies I look for, and I am willing to sift through the junk to find the timeless and true. We're all hoping to find an experience that awakens us. The movies that let us know we are alive and we have a purpose, a dream.

This is the rare type of conversation I had with my wife the other day. I cherish them. And like most of these moments, it was not planned or expected. I don't even remember what started the conversation. We were in a car, just the two of us. We started discussing God's will for our lives and how we know what it is. You know, it was the 'Am I doing what I am suppose to be doing in my life?' and the 'Is there more?' type of conversation. Then she made a statement that almost passed me by. She probably doesn't even remember making it. But in retrospect, I have found it to be priceless. It challenged my faith. It made me think. It was one of those rare statements that bring you face to face with God.

She said that we spend our lives *wanting* to do something for God and while waiting to do anything, we do nothing. In other words, it's the 'burning bush' or the 'I want to be a star concept.' Far too often we wait for God to send us a great, miraculous sign and we don't do anything until we get it. We waste our whole life *waiting* when we could be *doing*. "When God puts me on a stage in front of hundreds of thousands of people, then I'll give myself completely to Him." Until then, I'm in control. Or, one of my personal favorites, "When I am a millionaire, I'll start tithing." Hey, if we can't give ten cents out of our dollar, there isn't a chance of giving a hundred out of a thousand, or a thousand out of ten thousand, or…you get the point? It goes something like this:

A family prays and thanks God for the wonderful meal at the best restaurant in town, throws half of it away because they are full. Then they walk right by a man living on the streets, who hasn't eaten in days on the way out to their BMW.

A boy begs his mom for shoes that cost a hundred and fifty dollars, not because they will last longer than the forty-dollar pair, but because they have the really cool symbol on them. They are the same ones that all the popular kids are wearing. At the same time, an infant dies in a third-world country due to malnutrition; a tragic death, that for thirty dollars a month could have been avoided.

A woman passes the stranger at church, because she has to get with her 'circle of friends' to hear the latest Christian gossip (not so cleverly disguised as a prayer concern) about an affair, or marital problem, or alcohol addiction…ad infinitum /

ad nauseam. Feeling ostracized, that stranger never comes back to the church...never finds the welcoming grace and forgiving love of Christ.

Jesus puts it this way in Matthew 25:

> Come, you who are blessed by my Father; take your inheritance, the kingdom prepared for you since the creation of the world. For I was hungry and you gave me something to eat, I was thirsty and you gave me something to drink, I was a stranger and you invited me in, I needed clothes and your clothed me, I was sick and you looked after me, I was in prison and you came to visit me. Then the righteous will answer him,'Lord, when did we see you hungry and feed you, or thirsty and give you something to drink? When did we see you a stranger and invite you in, or needing clothes and clothe you? When did we see you sick or in prison and go to visit you?' The King will reply, 'I tell you the truth, whatever you did for one of the least of these brothers of mine, you did for me. Then he will say to those on His left, 'Depart from me, you who are cursed into the eternal fire prepared for the devil and his angels. For I was hungry and you gave me nothing to eat, I was thirsty and you gave me nothing to drink, I was a stranger and you did not invite me in, I needed clothes and you did not clothe me, I was sick and in prison and you did not look after me.' They will also answer, 'Lord, when did we see you hungry or thirsty, or a stranger or needing clothes or sick or in prison, and did not help you?' He will reply, 'I tell you the truth, whatever you did not do for one of the least of these, you did not do for me.'
>
> Matthew 25:34–45 (NIV)

I often catch myself dreaming of doing great things for God. I dream of being a champion of the faith; of being a David, or a Samson, or a Moses. Yet slowly, I am learning to be content where I am, just doing what I can right here, right now. If you want to change the world, start right where you are, with yourself, and then reach out to those close to you. If God wants to put me in the spotlight, then so be it. I pray that I give all the glory back to him. But if he wants me behind the scenes, then I pray that I will do the small tasks as best I can.

I don't dream of being a David anymore. Lord, just let me be a stone in the sling of David, used by you for your glory. May I be faithful in the little things, the daily, and the seemingly trivial. That is where we make the difference. I was once told that you can't steer a car if it isn't moving! You can turn the wheel until it hurts, but unless you put the car in gear, you aren't driving; you aren't going anywhere. We are a lot like that car, just waiting to move until God steers us. It doesn't make a whole lot of sense. We are supposed to live a life of faith. Let's *move* and trust that God will steer us, as we are open to Him! Of course, we have to be looking for him and avoiding things we know we ought to avoid. We also have to drive with common sense. But while I am waiting for God, while I am looking for God, let me do something, anything.

Life is but an instantaneous moment, and dreams fade without warning.

All is lost unless we discover the power of family and the strength of love.

a long dark snow storm of the soul

I could be working. I'm in my office. Work surrounds me. Yet, the only strength I can muster is spent watching the snow turn the world a uniform white. I love "winter rain." It's a storm, yet there is a peace that can be found within it; blissful tranquility. There is a beauty in a snowstorm that is missed by those who are too busy complaining about the cold or the condition of the roads. I would have missed this one myself, if I had been working.

There is no beauty in my office. It is a mess. It does, however, accurately reflect my life these past few weeks. It has been fairly crazy around here. My wife found out that she has to fit thirty hours of teacher observation into her schedule , and that's on top of her class overload. I was already over-booked when I found out that I had to prepare a sermon for next Sunday. I suppose I wouldn't be so far behind if I hadn't spent an entire day fixing the car. Now, thanks to my mechanical expertise, strange sounds greet me whenever I turn the key. And right smack dab in the middle of it all, a funeral. A funeral is like a bucket of ice water tossed on you while you are sleeping. It rudely awakens you to reality. It forces you to stand and face your own mortality. It can be shocking, even disheartening. But it doesn't have to be.

Sometimes I think I write more for myself more than for anyone else; to get things straight in my own mind. I write to capture a memory or maybe to reach a milestone. This keyboard is set for some pretty philosophical waters. The work that clutters my desk can wait.

Ah, the funeral. It wasn't nearly as sad as some. It was for a very dear lady. She was quite old, and with death came a peaceful release from the daily suffering caused by cancer. She had settled her affairs and said her goodbyes. Not a bad way to leave this world. It was her goodbyes that caught my attention. Memories of other funerals passed through my mind. Funerals have to be the biggest drawback to my work as a pastor. The tragic loss of someone young, a soul taken too soon, for no apparent reason. And the rest of us are left to feel the pain and contemplate the whys. You hear the stories everyday. They're all over the morning paper and the evening news. They all have a common theme: No last words. A college student is killed in a crash, and friends and family long to say 'I love you' just one more time. A baby is taken in the middle of the night, and the couple desperately seeks another chance. It is as if we hold our final words until it is too late. They become bitter poison in our mouths. What do you say when there is no one left to hear the words?

The storm outside my window is rivaled only by the one brewing within me. I think back over my life. How many opportunities did I let slip through my fingers; opportunities to speak the words while they could still have done some good? Why didn't I speak words of encouragement to someone in despair?

Should I have spoken words of comfort to someone in pain? Could I have spoken words of help to someone in need? How many times have I closed my heart's door and locked it tight with fear and pride? Does my family know that I love them and that I would offer my life for them? Does my mother realize that the summer I spent living with her meant everything to me? Or how thankful I am that I got a chance to truly get to know the person behind the title of 'mother'? Does my father realize how much it meant to me to see him at every single one of my sporting events? Most of the time, I sat the bench, which is sad considering it was only the intramural league. But he was there. And afterward he made time to play catch or grab a coke. Yes, I'm sure they know, but did I tell them myself? Telling them makes all the difference in the world.

I often think God goofed when he called me. I am a man of shortcomings and wayward intentions. My only comfort is in knowing that God is bigger than me. King David was known as a man after God's own heart. There is still hope for me. Hope, because I am alive, and with life comes learning. If I have never said all I needed to say, I say it now. Mom, Dad, I love you. I thank you for your support, love, and encouragement. Thank you for always being there for me. And that goes double for my wife, all my siblings, and my friends. I hope the memories we share express what words can never say.

I must wrap this chapter up, which means conclusion. Conclusion always involves summary. Let's see, the trend is to go to school, get married, get a job, and die. I think there is more, much more. I have learned that education and careers are noble pursuits and necessary for sustaining life. But family, friends, and love, that is the stuff that makes life worth living. I wouldn't trade parachuting out of an airplane or skiing in Colorado with my friends for anything. I wouldn't give up sleeping on the floor at my mom's the night before Christmas or camping with my dad and family for all the stuff the world has to offer. I would rather be an unknown man with a loving wife at my side and family and friends who are close to me, than be a famous and wealthy man, all alone. It's all in the definition of "rich" I guess.

So I encourage you to speak your final words while your heart is still beating. Life is crazy and can so easily get out of control. Sometimes we have to stop and watch the snow fall and smile at the storm. Just be thankful. It's still snowing. My work is still waiting. No one was saying a word. I just wanted to say something before the silence became permanent.

obsession, isolation, & rollercoasters

It's been a very long time, probably a little too long. I used to love them. I would stand in line for hours, just for the two and a half minute thrill of a rollercoaster. Now, now I just hate waiting. I still love the speed and the thrill. I can still hear the rhythmic clicking sound as the massive chain pulls the train up the first big hill. Then the eerie silence and a brief pause. Just long enough to make you wonder when it will start plummeting downward then…WHAM! Nothing but speed, the wind in your face and the hum of the track. Down, up, floating, jerking and lurching you from one side to the other, upside-down. Some rollercoasters even add the element of darkness, fog, or blinding strobe lights. Is it really worth the wait? Like most things in life, it's all a matter of perspective.

Even though I haven't had the pleasure of standing in line at an amusement park in a while, truth be told, I ride a rollercoaster every day. I wish it were in a park with the hot sun and those four dollar hotdogs, but it's not. My rollercoaster starts in the bedroom. It seems I step out of bed, only to be strapped into the front car. My life, my faith, my relationships are all one big rollercoaster. I spend most of my day trying to control the ride. Too many ups and downs and unsuspecting turns and twists.

I'm in the dark more than I'm in the light, and I have no idea where this thing is going. And for a little while, it's a great ride. Most of the time, however, I feel sick to my stomach and just want off.

Who built this ride anyway? How did I get belted into it? Where the heck is it going? And *when* is it over? Actually, I know the architect who designed the blue prints for this beast of a ride. *I* constructed it; every piece of steel, every bolt, with my own hands. I willingly climbed right in too. Although in all fairness to me, I didn't have a clue what I was getting myself into. I thought I was putting together a fun, safe ride. But my creation got away from me. I created a monster. It has transformed and has a mind of its own now.

It is a ride of intense extremes. I go back and forth from obsession to isolation. Up and down from ecstasy to apathy; love to hate; joy to sorrow; passive to aggressive; push to pull, happy to angry and every emotion inbetween. I better explain. I will attempt to paint a picture using two major areas of my life: faith and relationships.

Relationships. I think back over the years to a younger, thinner me, back in the days when I actually had to comb my hair. I remember my dating relationships. I was in love. I would do anything for the woman of my affection. My life read like a storybook romance, and I was out to win the fair maiden. She was my every waking thought. I would write letters every day, talk on the phone for hours and spend my whole paycheck on her. She consumed my world. If you've ever been in love, I know you know what I am talking about.

But obsession is a fairytale. It doesn't last. Reality killed the dragon, and the handsome knight woke up from his dream.

Life has a way of smacking you squarely in the face. You fight it, but slowly routine replaces adventure. "I can't live without you" is replaced with "Just leave me alone." Little disagreements become heated arguments, which turn into big, fat, ugly fights and before you know it, you wind up in isolation. Dazed, confused, disillusioned and alone. It is the tragic story of anyone who ever fell in love, only to have their happily ever after end in divorce court.

Somewhere between the fabulous fairytale and the dastardly divorce is the rollercoaster of good days and bad; trying and then giving up. Life brings hardships. Communication isn't easy. Love is work. Marriage; a full time job. Stress is the norm. Why? Does it have to be? Why do we jump from extremes so easily? Is it really an all or nothing proposition?

I do the same thing with my faith. There are days when I am obsessive about discipleship. I read scripture. I pray without ceasing. I try so hard to live a life worthy of the calling. I'm on fire; the mountain top; filled to overflowing; insert your own metaphor and I'm there. The very next moment, I'm just tired. I want a break. I just can't do it. I'm zapped, whipped, totally spent and considering throwing in the towel. Faith, like a rollercoaster, is no fun at all. Isolation from God is a very lonely place to be. And knowing that I am the one that put myself there only makes matters worse.

I have spent so much time wondering how I can be so close to God one minute and so far away the next. It's the same story with my marriage, my family, my friends, my job and on and on the rollercoaster goes. I love life, I hate life. I love my job, I want to quit. I relax, then I freak out. I think I am doing great, and then I trip and fall flat on my face. I am obsessive-compulsive. I love people, and then I just want to be left alone. Up and down, twist and turn, lurch this way and jerk back that way. I don't even know if I am right side up or upside down half the time. And all I really want to know is…

How Do I Fix It?

The best answer I can muster is this: I don't fix it because I can't. It is not fixable. Not completely, anyway. And the bottom line is, I don't want to fix it. Not really. We are human, and part of the package deal is that we are emotional, imperfect creatures. Balance is overrated anyway. Think about it. A perfectly balanced life with no highs or lows. Everything is planned. I don't want to live there, and neither do you. Passion and excitement; elation and ecstasy; love and peace; you can't have any of them without the other side of the coin. Pain and anger; turmoil and headaches, let's face it, if we never experienced the dark we wouldn't know how great the light can be.

But be very careful here. This is not license to live anyway you want. There are too many people living just for self, who are willing to hurt anyone that stands between them and their addiction to pleasure, power, controlled substances, you name it. This is not a call to live free of moral responsibility without regard to consequence. I am simply stating that as you strive to find perfection, cut yourself a break, because we won't find it on this side of heaven.

So now that we're on the same page and in agreement that we can't just do anything that feels good and justify it with a "Well, so what. I'm not perfect" attitude, we must also realize that there are many people who suffer from serious disorders, who have already lost control of the situation and may need professional help. Addiction to anything is a terrible place to live and, for some, can be impossible to battle alone. In these cases, professional help must be sought. The issue *I'm* trying to address is that elusive place between selfish immaturity and addiction/bondage that most of us would like to find.

Start by realizing that you are in control of your rollercoaster ride. Know in advance that there will be good days and horrible ones. Yes, we make good decisions, and we also mess up royally at times. No, we cannot control what life throws at us, but we can control how we respond to it.

When it comes to big-picture issues like family and faith, be prepared to work at it. Don't act like a disappointed child when success doesn't come overnight. Is it an all or nothing proposition? The muddy answer is yes and no. Yes, in the sense that you are either riding the rollercoaster or you are not. I choose whether or not to get in the seat. For example, if we choose marriage or parenthood, then we need to sit down, strap in, and enjoy the ride.

Communication, open, honest loving communication, is a beautiful thing. No matter the situation, communication has to be part of the answer. Not being much of a talker, I learned that the hard way. It is the same with God. When I entered the ministry, I made this promise: I promised God that no matter how many mistakes I made; how many times I fell, I would never give up if he would just hang in there with me. And he has kept his end of the deal. He has never given up on me, not once. Faith is a learning process. So if we don't get it right the first time or the second or the third, we have to keep going.

Keep going. We tend to give up, because we allow ourselves way too many outs. The idea that when things go sour in a marriage, the easy way out is to dump the whole thing and end it, is just crap. So your marriage is hard, welcome to marriage. They *all* are. The best things in life are always a challenge. That is part of what makes them great.

I have a two-year-old son that has slept through the night just one time in his life,–one. That's it. Let's do the math. Three hundred sixty five days in a year times two is seven hundred thirty minus one equals seven hundred twenty nine nights of frustration and sleeplessness. So what's a dad to do? Do I say, "Well this parenthood thing isn't working out like I thought it would, so I guess I will have to get rid of the kid." No, I think not. I love him. I love him with every breath that is in me. I love him forever, unconditionally! I tough it out and go the distance. Because in some twisted, mysterious way, I love him that much *because* he doesn't sleep through the night. He needs me, and I love him for it.

So make the marriage work. Pay the price. Work, talk, cry, try harder, pray, set goals and budgets, see a counselor, do whatever you have to do. Happy marriages don't come with the "I do," they come with years of problem solving, compromising, and clinging tightest when the big bumps make you feel sick to your stomach. But, and this is the thing we too often forget, it's worth it! I have never met a person who worked out a problem and then wished they hadn't.

There will be times you only give a half-hearted effort. There are times you may feel you are not mentally or physically capable of going on. And in those moments when you know you've blown it with God, or family or friends, own up to it, and just keep on going.

So what if life has its ups and downs? So, sometimes I obsess, and at other times I am at the end of my rope. I'm finally coming to terms with the fact that faith and relationships are terrific as well as tumultuous. I can admit that I am selfish at times. I do what I know I shouldn't do. That's because I am unfinished, rough, incomplete, a work in progress. So are you. The key lies within your own willingness to accept that in yourself and in others, and in your continual commitment to strive for improvement. So jump in, buckle up, hold hands and enjoy the ride. I've never ridden a great rollercoaster that wasn't a totally awesome, thrilling, and mind blowing experience. So make your rollercoaster great.

"Are those the bad guys, Daddy? Where are the good guys? What is war? Why are the bad guys so bad? I think the bad guys need someone to love them and teach them to be good. I hope the good guys win. Daddy, can I draw a thank you card for the good guys?

—Perfect wisdom and a three year old

When there are no words, our thank you lives on in the heart.

thank you

"Just one more story, Daddy?" The wide-eyed wonder of a young child beckons for a few more moments of day and play.

"Not tonight honey, it's late," I reply.

She tries to protest, but all she can muster is a yawn. I snug her in the covers cuddled in with teddy bears and Barbie dolls.

"Sweet dreams, baby girl, I love you."

"I love you too, Daddy. If I wake up can I come in your bed?"

"Yes honey, now go to sleep." I turn the light off and pause on the other side of the door, peering through the crack. The soft glow of the nightlight outlines my angel as she drifts off to sleep.

Sweet dreams. If only it were that easy. The innocent dreams of childhood have long disappeared for me and for America. In the twinkling of an eye, the American dream has become a gut-wrenching nightmare. I join my wife watching the news. I catch a tear in her eyes as the images of horror flicker on the screen. I think back to this morning. A beautiful, sunny day. Cool, fall was arriving. I love fall. The leaves changing, frosty mornings, clear night skies. Everything so peaceful. What a difference a moment makes.

"Turn on the TV. We're at war," the call came into my office.

We aren't at war, I thought to myself. No one would attack America. Then, I watched in disbelief as the Trade Center collapsed. And my reality, my world, collapsed right along with it.

"What happened, Daddy?"

It was my daughter's voice. She had stopped playing to stare at the images on the screen.

What happened? How do I explain it to a three year old when I can't even explain it myself? Before I could formulate an answer, she went on:

"Look, Daddy, fire trucks, just like the ones you ride in."

There they were, first on the scene: policemen and firefighters. In smoke-covered confusion, masses of people run out. The firemen go in, into their worst nightmare. They respond, they don't think. They don't think about their families waiting back home. My wife is all too familiar with sleepless nights of waiting and wondering; trying not to allow your mind to think the worst, to think of something like *this.* They don't think of their children. They just go. The rest of us are left to do the thinking, the dreading, and the praying. They just respond to the call.

We are at war! But right now the war is not waged on a field of battle. The enemy is not a country or political group. The war is not fought by trained soldiers in the military. The war is against death itself. The soldiers are the brave firefighters who boldly answer the call. They fight on through exhaustion and pain. They do what no one wants to do, but someone *must.* They risk their lives in the hopes that others might live.

Of the firefighters that went in, some were called to make the ultimate sacrifice. They gave their lives trying to save others. Their country screamed for help, and they answered with everything they had to give. I am reminded of the words of Christ, "Greater love has no one than this, that he lay down his life for his friends" (John 15:13 NIV).

I am a firefighter. I have seen fire; I have seen disaster; I know pain. What the men and woman responding in New York, Washington D.C., and Pennsylvania now face is more than fire and disaster. It is excruciating beyond imagination. It is nothing short of evil. Yet, they do not back down. They rise to the challenge, and they will be remembered.

I return to my daughter's room and kneel down next to her bed. I pray. I pray for the men and women who at this very moment risk their lives for others. I pray for the families of those who have given their lives. I pray for the little boys and girls whose daddies won't come home. I pray for peace. I thank God for those who faithfully serve, tirelessly work and fearlessly fight to save lives.

"What is that, Daddy?"

My daughter is pointing to my shirt. She rubs the sleep from her eyes. It is morning. She is looking at the small red, white, and blue ribbon that I wear. I bend down to talk with her, eye to eye.

"This, little girl, is the color of our flag." Before she can ask what a flag is, I continue on. "Our flag stands for freedom and peace. It means we all are created equal and should love one another."

"Why do you have it on your shirt, Daddy?"

"Yesterday," I tell her fighting back the lump in my throat, "yesterday that freedom was attacked. Many people were hurt and a lot of people died. I am wearing these colors to remember those people. It means I want to honor them and support them. Yesterday this happened, but today is a new day. Today, people all over the nation and the world are coming together and working side by side."

"To make it all better?" she asked.

"To make things better," I tell her.

"I wear these colors to support those working now, giving now, and serving now. And guess what, honey? Mommy made you one, too."

As I pin the ribbons on my baby girl's shirt, I can see pride on her face. I don't know if she understands any of this, but in her eyes there is love for today and hope for tomorrow.

I don't know if there is such a thing as a *good* war. I am sure that not every motive for war is pure. I love my country, even though she isn't always right. I want to make her better, stronger. The core is good. And those who defend her do so with honor. I stand in awe and I pray everyday, that I would live a life worthy of the sacrifices that gave me this freedom.

I ask you to remember those who lost their lives; support those who even now serve and reaffirm your call to live a life worthy of such sacrifice. Love your family, hug your children and pray. May we all return to the basics of love and peace.

You're asleep. It's late. It's dark. Suddenly, a piercing scream shatters your dreams. You stumble for the light only to see your spouse in a cold sweat, shaking.

"What is it?" you ask.

"It was terrible!" comes the reply.

"Bad dream?'

"Worse."

"You heard someone in the house?" you ask, becoming afraid.

"Worse. Much worse."

"Then what is it?"

"It's our son. I...I...I saw his future, and he's just like me."

-Conversation between any couple who has ever had children

mini me

"I love my children, but they freak me out!" It's like holding up a mirror. Not only do I see my eyes, my nose, my ears; but I also see myself. They look like me, talk like me, they act like me. In my offspring, I am reborn. My personality, my attitude; it's me inside and out. And that is what scares me. Will he grow up to be like me? Will he make the mistakes I did? When will he fall in love? What will he excel in? What will he do?

I never feared death. I did fear a painful death, but not death itself. Never, that is, until I had children. My son struck the fear of my own mortality in me. I actually sat up nights wondering if I would be around long enough to see him graduate from high school. Would I be there to watch him play sports or loan him my car for his first date, like my dad did for me? Would I be there for his wedding day or there to tell him how proud I am of his accomplishments? There to see my grandchildren? How long would I be there?

Children will change you. They cannot *not* change you. I swear, I could turn off the television and just watch my boy run around the living room. I would laugh the night away, because it's like someone shrunk me down and there I was. I can't believe the blessings he has brought to my life. The first hug, first dada, first high-five. Every first takes your breath away. And then… then you blink and it's over.

When I'm gone, my boy will be on his own. Does he know how painful it was to watch him make mistakes? Or get hurt? And how proud I was when he stood like a man and owned up to his mistakes and tried to make them right? So many nights I prayed that I could be a super hero to my boy; that I would be a great dad and bring him up right.

Truth is, 'right' is tough to define. Truth is my son has taught me more about life than I have taught him. He has taught me patience and how to lighten up. The list flows on like a river: character, hope, faith, love, peace, contentment, joy, all revisited in my son. Truth is, I am not the man I want to be. I am an unfinished and incomplete assignment. And while we are on the subject of truth, allow me to be honest: *This whole parenting thing scares me to death!* What if I'm not there when he needs me? What if I stumble? What if I mess up? What if I fail completely? And that's just the what ifs, don't even get me started on the whys. Too late. I'm already there. Why do I get so frustrated? Why can't I find more time? Why do I have to fall short over and over again?

What if, why, if only…welcome to parenthood. There isn't an owner's manual. And there's no way we'll get everything right. But as I watch my boy sleep, I smile. No, I'm not perfect and I don't get it all right all the time, but I know I got my son right. He is me, only a better, fresher, new and improved version. So much hope in his eyes. Young faith in his heart. Set a course for adventure, it's a brave new world and my boy and I have plans to explore.

I understand now. Understand more about my own parents. Hindsight and experience have a way of doing that to you. Maybe my parents weren't as crazy as I thought? (Nah, they're nutz!) Maybe there will come a day when I'm the crazy one and my son knows it all just like I did. Maybe I will survive his teen years. Maybe he will be a better me, take all the good and leave all the bad. That would be nice. Maybe, just maybe, I'll be able to get through to him. In one of those magical, mystical, teachable moments, maybe my son will see a hero in me. That's the biggest lesson my son has taught me, *maybe*. Life is full of maybes. Tomorrow is a new day and full of promise and hope. Anything is possible. He has taught me to let go of the past and live in the 'maybe' of today. I fully intend to enjoy every moment. After all, it's only a blink.

the greatest chapter...almost

In Defense of Bumps
an apologetic view of what was almost the Greatest Chapter.

In a general sense, the night was perfect. The temperature was in the mid-seventies with a cool breeze. Every star placed in the sky was shining with a fiery brilliance. The moon lit the earth in a dark blue haze. Shadows danced. Yes, the night was perfect, in a general sense.

It was a night to squeeze all the marrow out of life. Couples dotted the walk-ways and parks, and the dance clubs and restaurants were bursting at their frames. Oh, the farmers could have used a little rain but even the farmers couldn't help but to wander outside; even if they did grumble something under their breath as they retired for the evening. With fall closing in, bringing the onset of winter, this was a night to live. It was a night of love; of romance; of fun; of games; of laughter. Yet, something was different about this night. For one, it meant the end. This night could turn his world upside-down.

I awoke to the unfamiliar smell of stale, stagnate air. As I tried to focus, slowly, achingly, I turned over on the rented bed. Next to me, blanketed in the morning light, slept my best friend in the world. We grew up together. She was the keeper of some of the most meaningful memories in my life. Whether kneeling at the throne of heaven, or facing the gates of hell; standing like a man or weeping like a child; if I was apathic or energetic, she was there. She understood; better than me at times. What wrong turn did I make to end up here? The road ends where the heart and soul die. Is there a new path? One unseen? I stared at her for what seemed like forever. Memories flooded my mind. Tears filled my eyes as I reached up and felt the bumps on my neck.

Where was I? How did I get here? Last night, that perfect night, at least in my mind, I stood on the threshold of life and death. She was not like me. We started out the same and plans were made to stay that way. But plans fail.

She slept on peacefully. She would awake refreshed and rush back to reality. She would not notice that my life could have ended just a few hours before, while she slept. Something deep inside of me had snapped. I knew that the pieces were so shattered, that it would be impossible to put it back together. The trigger had been pulled, leaving nothing but a wounded soul. Now, all that remained was the question of whether or not to rebuild.

Confused? Me too. I guess I should start this story from the beginning; examine all of the issues in the morning light of truth. If the unexamined life is not worth living, then I am forced to reflect deeply upon the scads of worthless living I have already done.

I was born into an abnormal family situation and programmed to be normal. "Big boys don't cry." "Just keep it in." "Let no emotions show." "You've got it better than the other kids." With the faith of a child, I became a robot. I cried out at all the symptoms, ignoring the disease. No one heard my silent screams, and within my mind the battle escalated. My mind absorbed everything, but my heart felt nothing. Cold was the fact; normal was the front. I wore my scars like badges.

On my own, I learned that love was a noun, not an adjective: A terribly missued noun. Later, I discovered that love could represent many nouns: lust, sex, sin, perversion, and the most devastating lesson, nothing but an empty word, void of any real meaning.

While my subconscious soaked in the dirty little lessons that the world was teaching me, I struggled with another conflict, deep within the mire of my murky soul. Lost in despair, a faint voice cried underneath it all. It was the cry of faith. I had been taught how to play the *game* of Christianity. Yet even through my facade of faith, somehow, a part of me knew that there was much more than I realized, just waiting to be discovered.

I must back up farther again, not to the beginning of my life, but rather to the beginning of this chapter in my story. It is now 2:33 a.m. I am in college. It is Saturday morning (or Friday night, depending on how you look at it.). At any given time, it seems I am always tired. I hold down three jobs, am facing taking my midterms completely unprepared, and on top of it all, I have these strange, unexplained bumps on my neck. In the last four days, I have managed to get in six hours of sleep. I am a walking zombie and I don't care. That's the most significant confession I'll ever make: I don't care! Then I spout off and tell you about the pressure of midterms and that I am overworked at my jobs, all for the sake of piety and pride. Sorry, but it works for me, at least at this point in my life.

People look at me and say, "What a Christian." It's because I know what buttons to push, to make them respond as I want them to. It's an endless con-job. Sometimes, Christians are the easiest people to lie to and to fool. I guess I really wasn't *lying*. I was simply using my unfortunate circumstance to my advantage. Or, at least that's what I told myself.

I decide to turn in. It will be Saturday when I wake, and I have a date with an old friend. It's 3:30 a.m., and I still can't sleep. As I stare out the window, endless questions float through my head. What will it take to change my life? I feel like I am going nowhere, *fast* and I don't care. The irony is that everyone *thinks* that I have it all together. Maybe these bumps on my neck are the answer. Let me explain.

Last week, I noticed little bumps on my neck. They grew and began to hurt. I went to the campus nurse. She didn't have any idea what they could possibly be. (Which proves she is a nurse.) Poison ivy, hives, enlarged glands, they could be anything. So, I am referred to a doctor who gives me drugs and a large bill. (Which proves he is a doctor.) The drugs do nothing for the bumps, and the doctor starts to worry. He wants a blood test. He says it is routine and not to worry, but then decides to add that it *could* be cancer. Cancer! He uses the word as if it were completely void of any significance.

"Oh and by the way, you could have a fatal disease, but don't worry too much because we don't know yet."

Thanks, doc. You moron! What does he care? He deals with death everyday. He is immune. But in a strange way, I am immune too.

I told no one of the bumps that ran along my neckline. When they became noticeable, they began to draw questions.

Reciting the well rehearsed, "just swollen glands," would usually do the trick and shut off any further debate on the subject. But cancer? That haunting thought lead me to just one question. What's the deal with this game called Christianity that I learned to play so well as I was growing up? Could there be more to it than I realized or wanted to admit?

It's funny how clear hindsight becomes when you have a focal point like the prospect of cancer staring you in the face. Staring right back at me, the ugly mess my life was in; all the people I had hurt. Suddenly, my priorities began to shift like a landslide. Good grades didn't matter. My jobs and the money I was making didn't either.

"Would all family, friends, and important memories head quickly and directly to the top of the priority list, please?" ordered my sub-conscious. All inhibitions were lost. I guess that is where I got the nerve to ask my old friend out; to confess a crush I had felt for her that had never been revealed, before it was too late.

Still trying to drift off to sleep, my mind wandered over the events of the day. I had slept through my first class. It was the only hour of sleep I had managed to catch in twenty four hours. I awoke just as class ended, then groggily headed into chapel. I remember the speaker talking about a big faith, a faith that ventures out into the real world. Real world? Is there such a place? Everyone makes reference to this mysterious place, but no one seems to know where it is. And as far as faith goes, I'm having a tough enough time with my fake faith, without even trying to tackle any kind of "big faith." Oh, sure, I have dreams of a big faith…Someday, just not right now.

I immediately identified with the speaker as he uttered these words, "I want a life and death faith. I want my Christianity to be a matter of survival, not a matter of taste."

I had done a great deal of tasting in my twenty or so short years of life. But how do you find *a life and death faith?* Maybe God had decided to expedite the search for me, in the form of cancer. I felt my neck again, realizing that I could no longer deny the thought I had struggled with all day long.

"Fine, God. I hope I do have cancer. Bring it on! Part of me actually wants this damned disease," raged my conscience.

Don't misunderstand me. I don't believe I have a death wish. But if you think about it, hoping for cancer is not as insane as it sounds. It simply requires a different perspective. But if I had anything going for me at all, it was perspective. Cancer would instantly force me to find a real faith. I could live as a Christian and everyone would look up to me. I could almost die as a martyr among my friends and family. All of the mistakes and failures of my life would be forgotten. It's not so hard to live for God when he is all you have left, and you only have to do it for a little while. Anyone can fake it for a short time. Maybe my greatest fear was that the bumps would actually go away. Then I would have no choice but to find God on my own.

Sometimes I think I'm a Christian because it sounds nice, looks good, and because it gets me attention, not because I need to be. Oh, that I might just once need Christianity. Need it, like you hear about missionaries who need it: Need it like the air you breathe! A faith that can only come as a result of a changed life, that is what I am looking for. A life freed from sin; redeemed and bought, dead to the world and alive in Christ. Now would someone please tell me, *how do I get there?*

Sometimes I want to leave everything: school, friends, church, jobs, everything. People did it all the time in the sixties. I would just start walking across America. No money, but no bills. No home, but no commitments. I would be on my own and completely available and open to discover my own faith. Maybe then it would be necessary instead of nice. It would also get me out of this pathetic college. Out of the mold everyone seems determined to squeeze me into. It would force people to deal with the real *me*, and destroy all of my other false-faces. We wear our masks; we hold our shield. What if I just ripped the mask off and threw the shield down? Forget about the consequences. What could they do? What would it do to my faith?

Back to my story. The collegiate day dragged on. It was an unconscious routine: a blurring ritual of meaningless trivia. My thoughts were fixated on nothing but my date. Ceremoniously, I went through the preparation for the big night. I washed and waxed the car and then showered and shaved with precise care. Finally, it was time to pick her up.

The evening was going well. We were having a great time. We always did whenever we were together. It was one of those relationships that could have been more, but the timing was always off. We had no social expectations to hinder us. We'd known each other way too long for that. The dating games and false fronts that people put up to impress each other were never there for us. We talked, we laughed; it was completely unpretentious and comfortable. We just fit. This was turning out to be the perfect date.

Then something went wrong; terribly wrong. Somewhere on the way to a dinner and a movie, the conversation shifted, and we began to discuss whether or not it was possible for a man and woman to 'just be friends.'

Somewhere along the way, I confided in her about my 'bumps.' We talked not of cancerous bumps but of spiritual bumps. What would it take to get both of us into a real relationship with God? What would my 'bumps' turn out to be? I confessed to her and to myself, that if I did have cancer, I would not be transformed into a spiritual giant. I would become a scared child.

No, cancer was not the answer. Slowly, I realized that what I was really looking for, were the 'bumps' that would break the chain and put an end to the sick-cycled carousel of fake-faith, once and for all. Somehow I didn't imagine that it would be a big bump. It would be a series of daily struggles and no one was going to hand it to me on a plate. I had to find my *own* way to wake up the dormant faith within me.

"The road ends where the heart and soul die." Is there a new path? One unseen? I headed back to college with a strange sensation that maybe there was. No one was going to do it for me. I had to get *myself* to the place where God could take over completely. Most of our growing takes place in the valley, but there is a time to climb the mountain, in order to reach new valley floors.

My neck doesn't hurt as much anymore.

"Editor's edit, it's what they do"

This was going to be the greatest chapter I had ever written. Not greatest in terms of literary genius or long acceptance speeches at award banquets. Great as in honest, true, gut-level openness. A real chapter that tears off the mask, stops the pretending and just throws it all out there. Put the cards on the table, and calls a spade a spade.

But then my editor got a hold of it. The message was clear: "Are you kidding? This is much too revealing," was the reaction. "You can't just candidly, blatantly, throw temptation and struggle and sin into a chapter! This is supposed to be a *Christian* book," reprimanded the editor.

There was no sugar-coating and no warning.

"*No, no, not acceptable.* Being that open and honest would be the death of any hopes of getting published. The chapter, exactly as you wrote it, would be "R" rated, at best. Why don't we just axe the whole thing and start again?"

Editors. Sheez! What do they know? I tried to see the point that was made (in the form of censorship), and my rational side *did* know the editor was probably right. No sense in airing dirty laundry and secrets of the past in a book. But this was supposed to be a book about life. Not just my life, mind you, but all life; my life, your life…and life is filled with the worst of struggles and temptations. Life is lived in the midst of choices. Some are good choices and some, well, sometimes we just plain blow it and blow it big. I struggle. I fall. Often. I am in need of grace and forgiveness. My life is "R" rated at best; more like "NC17" at times. There are battles that rage within and without everyday. Why can't we just acknowledge that fact and talk about them?

So, sorry for the gaping space and blank pages, but this is all that is left of the chapter. It is incomplete and filled with holes. It stays in the book, however, because it is a true representation of real life. We are incomplete and filled with holes. We need grace and yes, at times censorship, I suppose.

This was going to be a great chapter!

"Distorted, hideous, always hidden. It plagues millions and is talked about by almost no one. Those who do speak are labeled and tucked away by society. So, it rages out of reach, out of hope hidden behind the eyes…it is a battle of the mind."

dead grass
A Parable

Whatever happened to sin? It just doesn't seem to be politically correct to talk about it anymore. We can talk about religion and engage in conversation regarding beliefs, as long as the conversation remains on the surface level. But sin is never a surface level topic. *Discreet gossip* is okay, but the transgression itself never really gets labeled *sin*. Society just doesn't like to use that word.

The news and tabloids are filled to the brim with the stuff, but it's written off as a mistake, a misunderstanding or given some other entertaining spin. The problem is, when we put our own 'spin' on sin, those who are struggling with it have nowhere to go. Secret sin claims too many lives, and there just isn't enough help out there.

Since we are not allowed to talk about it, I offer instead, a story about my grass.

I was working in my yard. It was hot and I was tired, but I worked on. My yard was large, too large for one person to groom. I enjoyed my yard, though. I loved seeing the healthy green grass. I would have liked to do more, but there was the family and the church, and time was my most prized possession.

It was peaceful in the yard, alone. Something about working with your hands and seeing something grow just felt right. I'm not one of those obsessive folks with the underground sprinkler system and pricey chemical fertilization treatments. *Those* are the yards that rival most golf courses. I didn't have anything against those yards, mind you. I would have loved to have a yard like that. I was just too thrifty to pour that kind of money into it. So I mowed and I trimmed myself. I fertilized and I watered with my hose occasionally. I wouldn't have won any prizes, but I kept it up and it looked good. It reflected my life. I wasn't out to win a prize. I just wanted to do the best I could with what I had.

Then, it happened overnight, without warning, or so I thought. I woke up to a beautiful day. It was much too nice to spend the day in the office, so I got an early start hoping to cut out of work and get in nine holes with a friend. I walked outside and there it was, in the shade of the old maple; a big, ugly brown patch of dead grass. It covered half my yard! What happened? Too much fertilizer? Did I spill gasoline? Miffed, I kicked at a rock and found my answer. Under the rock only inches out of sight, lying just beneath the surface, I found slimy, life-robbing grubs.

There were no warning signs until it was too late. By the time I knew I had *grubs*, I had already lost half my yard. From the top view, my yard looked healthy. But underneath, it was being destroyed. All of my mowing and watering and fertilizing had been a waste of time. I was ignoring the very creature that was robbing my grass of its roots, its nutrients and its life. By the time I could see there was a problem on the surface, it was too late. I was left with dead grass. How long had the problem existed? No one knew. If only I had checked for them earlier. A twenty dollar bag of pesticide would have saved my green, green grass, but now it was dead, gone.

It was so much work and it cost me more than I ever dreamed it would, but I fought the grubs until I had a yard again. The process was a nightmare. I had to treat the grubs and prepare the soil and plant new seed and water it everyday. I battled seed-stealing birds and too much rain. Weeds grew with the grass, but the grass was too young to risk pulling the weeds, so I waited. Then it came in a different shade of green and I had to be patient for two whole seasons before it looked normal again. Things were finally looking up. I got my green grass back, and I was proud that I managed to keep most of the weeds out too. I learned a lot about grass and my yard that summer. After that episode, I treated for grubs every year. Prevention proved to be cheaper than allowing them to roam wild, then dealing with the damage later. Sure, it was a little more work, but ended up being much less trouble in the long run. It's too late to go back and change the past, but at least I learned from my dead spot and kept it from happening in my yard again.

And now for the moral of the story: I fully realize that we still can't talk openly about sin in our lives, so let me explain a few things about my yard. Each and every one of us has grubs. It is a fact of life. No one has ever lived a grub-free life. My advice is simple; if your grass is green, do whatever it takes to keep it that way. "An ounce of prevention…" as the saying goes. If you have some dead grass, it will never be any easier to deal with than it is right now. It will be hard work. Brown, dead grass sticks out and it is embarrassing and humbling, but you are not alone. There is help out there. Don't listen when society tells you to keep your grass problems to yourself. That is exactly what the grubs want. New life is just around the corner. Do the work and kill the grubs. A green grass life is worth it.

Nothing

I am sure of nothing.
I feel nothing.
Nothing is a constant companion.

Life can change in a moment.
How many moments do we waste? If change is inevitable, when will I change enough to believe and believe enough to change?

Let Go of Everything
or Hold onto Nothing

nothing

I hate these stupid things. What's the point? I paced nervously with one hand, holding the hospital gown together behind my back. I hate this place; so cold and sterile, uncomfortable.

"Simple. Routine," the doctor assured me. "Done it a million times before!"

I was not assured. There is nothing simple or routine about being cut open; being exposed. It's not that I was scared of dying. Sure, anything could happen, but we tend to live with the idea that it only happens to the next guy; the other family, certainly not me. Still, I was nervous. Being cut open has to hurt. How much pain is there going to be? How many people have to know? Will I be scarred? What will others think? Maybe that's why I don't fear death. I'm so afraid of living with pain and rejection and scars, that death doesn't bother me all that much.

I'm hungry! I wish I had food! How much longer? I glanced at the clock on the wall, soon. That old clock has been my constant companion. How many hours have I stared at a clock watching the rhythmic tick of the second hand? Those seconds have ticked away days of fear and dread. The closer it got, the more I thought. *Can I really go through with this? Am I ready?*

Am I strong enough? Can't I put it off a little while longer? I don't really feel that bad all the time.

The problem is that I don't feel much of anything anymore…I just…I…I can't even put it into words. It's like I'm sleepwalking most of the time, just numb to the pain. Numb to everything and everyone around me.

Will this surgery really work anyway? Others have had it done, but will it work for me? What will it cost? I don't have much. This could easily take everything I have. Am I willing to go that far? I could just live like this. Avoid the pain. Avoid the hassle. Avoid the cost. Avoid this stupid gown. Avoid everything. What if I don't go through with it? How will my life change? Can I get better on my own? I've been trying for years. No, it doesn't work. I've been struggling forever, and I'm sick and tired of being sick. I want out of this handicapped lifestyle. I want to be well, no matter what the cost or how much it hurts. If it takes everything I have, so be it! I'll risk it all, even death, because this is no way to live.

I sat down and prayed for strength. I opened my eyes to a blinding light. I was forced to shut them again. I squinted and tried to look, just a little this time. Everything was different. The light was so intense, it hurt and I couldn't focus. My surroundings were unfamiliar. It didn't feel like a hospital, but I could feel. I could feel! I wasn't numb, I wasn't sleepwalking. As my eyes began to adjust, my mind began to clear. I remembered the weeks of searching. I remembered the pain and emptiness that I carried. It had all led me here.

Suddenly, I realized why this cold, sterile place looked so familiar. It was the old country church I grew up in. Service was about to start. It had been cold and sterile all these years because I never understood. I never had the eyes to see past the religion. Why was today different? Why had I gotten up so early? Something within woke me up and told me to come. All I knew to do was pray. It was the first honest prayer I have prayed in a long time. "Help me, Lord." That was it. That's all I could muster over and over again.

Jesus spoke in parables. The Bible speaks of visions. Could it be that the hospital wasn't a dream, but a vision? Is this what it's like to hear from God? I looked down. I was no longer wearing that embarrassing gown. I realized what it represented. It was my old self: The sin, the guilt, the shame and the pride. I threw it all down. The fear was gone. I walked in and laid myself on the altar. I wanted to be well, and I knew I couldn't do it on my own. I needed the Great Physician. Only God could heal me, restore me, make me whole. I confessed my disease, praying freely now. I knew the operation would hurt, letting go of self is never easy, but I also knew it would be a complete success.

blinded by sight

Her name is Jaclyn and although she's only in middle school, she's one of my heroes. Jaclyn was born with a degenerative eye disease. She's grown up gradually losing her sight, always knowing that one day she will be completely blind. Jaclyn has had to face problems and pressures that most of us could not, at least not with the same maturity and strength. Did we even have any real problems back in the sixth grade?

I do not wish to describe Jaclyn as a Hollywood superstar-type hero. No, she is a real person with issues and fears. And even though she is scared of being blind, this young student lives life. Eventually, she will know what it is like to be without many things, but she will never know a day unloved. Her family models what 'family' ought to be. And I am humbled by their love and strength as I have become closer to them.

The intent of this chapter is not to tell you about Jaclyn's blindness. Rather, it is to tell you about yours. As it turns out Jaclyn can see things many of us 'sighted' folks cannot. In a strange twist, too often it is you and me who are the blind ones. If there is pity to be bestowed, then we must bestow it upon ourselves.

How many times do we miss what is real because we are living by 'sight'? How many times do our eyes play tricks on us? Jaclyn knows a faith deeper than most adults.

It is a faith that can only be born out of wrestling and struggle. It is not a faith of convenience. She has learned how to look within and examine herself, and how to listen. She is able to judge a person on heart and soul, not appearance. She has spent time being still.

I spent a couple of days blindfolded as part of a college experiment. It changed me. It changed my perspective and my world. Mine was a limited view. I could remove the blindfold anytime I wanted. It's not the same.

Jaclyn still invites me into her world whenever she gets a chance. We went rock climbing on an indoor wall a few months back, and she waited while I went up, and then challenged me to do it again, "her way." As I struggled up the wall without the use of my eyes, I began to 'see' things differently. I saw with my ears and my hands. I saw myself and my lack of trust in others. I saw my self-reliance and independence. I saw how much I take for granted every single day of my life.

As Jaclyn invited me into her world, now I invite you. Spend some time with your eyes closed. Reflect on your life. Look inside, instead of on the surface. Identify and "own up" to your own blindness. It is a difficult, often painful process. But a necessary one on the road to maturity. Address your blind spots, preconceived ideas, and prejudices. Take some time to get to know someone who isn't like you; someone of a different race or culture; someone with a handicap or of a different religion. Open your heart and your mind. Build a relationship and learn from each other. You'll be glad you took the time. Who knows, you might even find a hero. I did.

secrets

"I've got a secret. I won't tell. I promise. I won't. *Shhh!* It's a secret! You can't tell a soul. Now swear on it."

Children love secrets. For the most part, they are fun and innocent. Surprise birthday parties, Christmas gifts, not telling anyone the gender of your unborn child. But there is an uglier, darker side to secrets. Too many adults have extensive experience in this department. Secrets can control you, define you, own you and even destroy you.

I know what it's like to live with secrets. I'm guessing you do too, or at least you did at some point in your life. Secrets. They start out innocently, they make you feel alive, if only for a short while. A seemingly meaningless flirtation, one drink at a party, a fun trip to the casino, a suggestive magazine or video, and everything is fine; completely under control. Addiction and affairs are born of "innocent excitement" and "harmless fun." I have never met an alcoholic who woke up one day and made the conscious choice to become dependent on his favorite drink. The drug addict began simply by seeking an escape. The pornography junkie only wanted release. Pain and emptiness is a short walk from meaning and ecstasy. Just one wrong turn, that's all it takes. Secrets can be a lonely way to live.

What's your secret? Hard to say isn't it? Not just because it is a secret, but because if you live with it long enough, it takes on a life of its own. It's difficult to put into words. Knowing when, why, and how it began somehow gets tangled in your mind. My secret began much too early. I was only a child. Love was not an easy thing for me to understand, and even more difficult to express. I was the product of multiple divorces and the baby of the family, love was not an easy thing for me to grasp. Words never came out right. Messages were always mixed. I witnessed and existed in the gray area of "love."

Love

Obsession   Fear

Pride   Fights

Lust

Hurt

Trust

Passion

Adoration   Affection

I closed down. I refused to feel. I became a shy introvert, not knowing how to speak, share, or communicate. My secret pain almost destroyed me. There were several key moments and caring people that rescued me, guided me, and coaxed me out of my protective shell. They taught me how to express my emotions, how to love, how to live.

Why do secrets have to be so secretive? Don't we all mess up from time to time? Aren't we all just trying to figure out this thing called life? Don't we all hurt sometimes? If it's true that we can't go back and start over, then how do we make amends? How did choices of a frightened boy dictate the course of a man's life? How can you keep the past in the past? Humans aren't perfect, yet we expect perfection from each other, silly. Seems a waste of precious time. Maybe *perfect* is not a result of flawlessness, but rather a state of openness. If I declare my flaws to others and ask for help, and if others would suspend harsh judgment and criticism long enough to give it, there would be no need for secrets. We call that growth, maturity, honesty, character, life. Isn't God the perfect model of this concept? Our creator is the only one I know who suspends judgment and lovingly invites us into his arms. There are no secrets with God. He knows us and loves us just as we are, and then encourages us to grow and mature. We all need God and we need each other. At least one other…

There is one. That one precious soul who knows me, all of me. She has seen the best and the worst; the light and the darkness in me. She took me by the hand and guided me, held me, laughed with me and cried with me. A glance from her still steals my breath. She has brought about more growth than anyone else in my life. She brings out my creativity, inspires me, and gives me wings. Why? Because she knows me and still loves me. It's as simple as that. Unconditional love. It truly is the greatest of things.

I try to live without secrets now-a-days. It's not always easy. I suppose it's a process that we die trying to perfect. In the end, we grow and share and risk. I encourage you to risk. Risk opening yourself up to someone. The stakes are high, but the rewards are worth it. Harboring secrets is a miserable way to live. Honesty is liberating.

"I hate my job!"

                -confessions of pastors everywhere

confessions

No! That can't be right! People stuck in low paying dead end work hate their jobs! People who long for something more, people who hold tight to a dream they are not living hate their jobs. Pastors don't hate their jobs. Pastors are, well…nice. Pastors don't *hate*. They are dependable, solid, completely together. They *can't* hate, can they? Besides, what do they really do? How hard could it be? I mean I wouldn't want to get up in front of people and speak, but other than that, what is there, really?

Let me paint a picture for you. It will not be a work of art, but I trust it will be easily understood. I will call this picture, "My resignation."

Dear board of elders, church council, trustees, and congregation, I respectfully submit my resignation as your pastor. I have tried to serve faithfully over the years but came up wanting and tired. Tired of dealing with petty, meaningless issues that demand my every waking moment.

And just for the record, I don't care if there are cigarette butts in the parking lot or food in the church refrigerator without a name on it. I am sick of trying to be everything to everyone while being a stranger to God. I am tired of trying to please everyone with no time to explore what would please God. Tired of people sitting in the same pew and talking to the same people while the unchurched newcomer goes unnoticed. Tired of being type-cast into a mold that is not me, nor do I ever want it to become me. I am tired of the institutionalized, sterile setting, where there isn't enough time, money, or heart to do what God has called us to do. I'm tired of wearing a mask that proclaims that I have it all together. I don't. I struggle. I am a man and believe it or not, I struggle with faith, family, and life—just like you. At least I want to struggle. I am not afforded the opportunity to be real as your pastor.

So, there you have it. I want more. More of a faith than just this church. More love, more grace, more understanding, peace, patience, and hope than I experience now, in my church family. I want to find the great adventure promised when I began this journey. I want to be excited about coming to work, and at the end of the day I want to feel as if I have made a difference to those around me. I want to be part of a team in ministry. I want to be part of a community that has given itself over to something bigger than it could possibly imagine. I want to exercise my faith without fear of never being allowed to fail.

I trust you will have no trouble finding a suitable replacement for me as I am sure there are several pastors looking for the security of a church where nothing is expected to change and where updating the Sunday School Curriculum is seen as a major milestone. Someone out there must want to spend his days keeping the peace and steadying the boat. There are pastors out there that want to build a wall protecting those inside the church from the world at large. There are pastors willing to preach safe, happy sermons and never ask difficult questions. I am just no longer willing to be one of them. It is impossible for me to separate my professional life from my personal life. I want to be whole, integrated, and complete.

With regret,
Your pastor

The saddest part of this picture is what might have been. It didn't have to be this way. It could have been a beautiful masterpiece with vividly bold colors. A portrait that inspired all those who looked at it.

It still could be, I think. It's not too late. What would it take? It would take forgiveness and grace. The church would have to be willing to become a caring community. It would take a major move of God. We would have to seek Him and pray until we discovered what God wanted to do through us right now. Then, of course, we would have to be willing to do it. It would also take a church willing to ask tough questions and not give simple answers. We could start right now, you and me together, if you wanted to. Are we willing to try?

it's not about me

Well maybe just a little about me…
It could be about me…
But it shouldn't be…
I'm going to the mall.

I am obsessed with gadgets! My friends call me Techno-man or Gadget-guy; my wife calls me crazy. I love things! I was one of the first to put my daily planner onto a palm pilot, only to turn around and buy a cell phone that had the palm pilot built into it. I love iPods and jump drives. I bought a mini keyboard for my phone to send email from anywhere. I have a GPS unit and a wireless network in my house so I don't have to walk downstairs to use the computer. (Except now, I have to get on the treadmill because I am not getting enough exercise.) I own a DVD recorder with hard drive for my television and a universal remote that controls all things electrical.

Did I mention the multi-tool? (That's an upgrade from the Swiss Army knife.) From the sonic mole chaser in my yard, to flashlights for your head, and reading lights that clip on your ear, to the flip down screen in the van so my kids can watch Sponge Bob, I have tried them all. My favorite stores are Best

Buy and Brookstone. I am thinking about opening a "Gadgets R Us"!

I have a feeling that I am not alone in my passion for the newest and coolest 'things.' I am sure there must be more people like me out there than I realize. Stuff, whether it's electronic gadgets or clothes, stuff for the home or stuff for the office, we live in a culture that is addicted to stuff. It seems America has confused *wants* with *needs*. Don't get me wrong, I like stuff. Stuff isn't bad, until it takes on a life of its own.

I had a wise college professor who once told me that the computer program Quicken is a great tool. Not for keeping track of your financial records, though, that's just how they market it. But rather, it's great for keeping your spiritual life in check. He told me that whatever you spend the most time doing, the most time thinking about, the most money on, that is your god. That's no good! He is suggesting I worship my computer. He may be more right than I care to admit.

Can *stuff* really become a problem? I have a friend whose family sponsored a child with Compassion International. It's a great charitable cause with very little financial investment, something like thirty bucks a month. But she actually let the sponsorship go because she felt like it was 'infringing' on the things she could buy for herself and family. Hers was not a case of living paycheck to paycheck or wondering where the next meal was coming from, either. She could have afforded half a dozen sponsored kids without a financial strain. Now before you judge too harshly, stop and ask yourself what you are doing. Hers is the *rule* not the *exception*. Spending is an addiction, and most of us are guilty of it.

How do we find the balance? How do we know if we have a problem? First, I think we need to get at the real issue. I love the disease / symptom analogy. If I have a disease that is making me sick (let's say fever and great pain) then I can take some pain medicine and feel better. The problem is, I only treated the symptoms. The disease remains intact, continuing to do damage. The symptoms are there to let me know there is a deeper, more serious issue that I need to deal with. Once the pain medication wears off, I still have pain. If, however, I treat the *disease*, the pain and fever will go away.

Our obsession with spending money and owning stuff is the symptom. We need to look past that and get at the root cause. Do you spend when you are unhappy? Do you buy to keep up with the Jones'? (Where did the Jones' get all their money, anyway?) Is shopping a temporary fix to make you feel better? Are you compulsive?

Is your spending causing financial strain: unpaid credit cards, spending paychecks before they arrive? Or are you just selfish? Is it truly all about you and what you want? Not *need*, but want?

Why would I put a chapter that is so offensively obtrusive in here anyway? Am I just trying to give you a guilt trip? Could I be jealous? Think what you will, I'm dead, remember? Oh and here is the thing about being dead. I didn't get to bring any of my cool gadgets with me. (Which is unfortunate, because I bet that multi-tool would have come in handy.) There is no cell phone signal under this much dirt, plus the stupid mortician glued my lips shut, so I can't talk anyway. Okay, so death has made me a tad sarcastic. It's only because I missed the point while I was still stealing oxygen and replacing it with carbon dioxide. It was so simple to see. How did I miss it? I even read it on bumper stickers and never even got it. Right there on that rusted out Reliant K car in front of you. It's even in plain English:

"He Who Dies With The Most Toys, Still Dies"

Let me ask a few questions now that I should have asked myself before now:

- Did that stuff make me happy, really happy, we are talking lasting happiness?
- How much more time could I have spent with my children if I wasn't wasting time playing with my gadgets or watching my big screen television or working like a dog to pay for all that stuff?
- How many times did I say, "In a minute dear" and go back to my 'toys'?
- How much did all that stuff cost me? And not just in financial terms.
- How many people could I have helped if I wasn't so selfish?
- If I had it to do over, what would I do differently?
- Don't get me wrong, I think I was a pretty good guy. It's just that…well perspectives change. The most important stuff in life isn't stuff at all. There I said it. You read it. Now what?

the people in the white houses

Let me tell you about my friend, Steve. My first encounter with this long-haired freak was during my freshman year in college. Steve changed the way in which I viewed people forever. Like Jaclyn, he taught me not to judge the heart by what is seen. Steve's physical appearance can best be described by…well, by going to a circus and paying your two bits to see the side show just inside the tent. Oh alright, he wasn't quite that bad, but in a sea of Christian liberal arts students, Steve certainly caught you off guard. At first, I avoided him. Honestly, he was quite intimidating. Then came the day when I walked out of my room and into the hallway, and there he was, right in front of me. I couldn't avoid him without being obvious. As I walked toward him, I took in his outfit. Ripped jeans, multicolored bandannas tied around his legs, arms, and head. The unwashed, long eighties style rocker hair and the skull earrings definitely stood out. So did the faded leather bomber jacket and the fish net shirt, which covered an old concert tee-shirt that smelled like yesterday's cigarettes. His outfit could make any professor at our small, conservative, Christian college cringe. And just to push anyone else over the edge, he wore an electric guitar strapped to his back. He never went anywhere without that guitar.

Steve's appearance was outdone only by the company that he kept. What a way to begin your freshman year. As I passed him in the hallway that day, not knowing what else to do, I gave him the cool head nod that said, "Hey, what's up?" And he actually stopped right there, and started talking to me! I couldn't believe he was talking to a small town preppie like me. In fact, he seemed more accepting and approachable than most people I know, most *Christians* I know.

To my surprise, Steve and I became good friends. We took countless road trips together. My favorite expedition was to Hell, Michigan to visit a girl that he liked. We both took too much pleasure in telling everyone we saw on campus that we were going to Hell for a girl. Beside the road trips, we would skip class on the boring lecture days, in search of an education you couldn't find in the classroom. The kind that comes only from living life, meeting strangers, and venturing outside your comfort zone. I discovered that while Steve may have been a rebel without a clue, he was one of the most talented, intelligent young men I had ever met. He saw things that most Christians missed; things that most of us really need to see. With his permission and yours, I will share a short story that Steve wrote during our college days.

The People in the White House
A short story by Steve Evoy

A small town, a big church, and a college. Two streets away from the big church and the college in the center of the small town were the white houses. The people that lived in the small town knew about the white houses, as did the people in the church, and the people at the college.

The white houses were a spectacle, something about their lawns and their cars made the town think of runny noses and nicotine. Something about the dark windows and the battered doors made the people in the church nervous, as they clung to their addictive opiates of hymns and sports coats and handshakes every Sunday. The people in the college were somehow unable to speak about them—those dirty houses with weeds and cheap curtains. There were murmurs of removing the houses, condemning them and allowing the occupants to move along. The small town and the church and the college wanted the clean streets of their dreams. No one ever thought the houses had already been condemned, the occupants dehumanized; sadly, no one ever thought.

All the while, the people in the white houses lived in the shadow of the church and the school, perhaps they were lonely. It didn't matter, because some of them smoked and that was bad.

The town went about the business of towns. The church went about the business of churching and singing. That's okay, that's what towns and churches do for a living.

But the college was different; it realized the need to help people. Swelling with humility and bursting with piety, the college organized long trips to distant lands to see people in garbage dumps. This was good, because most people in garbage dumps have never seen walkmans before. The college drove vans into cities and put up pictures of all the dirty people they were touching.

All the while the people in the white houses watched. The college brought in guitars and drums, and they all clapped hands for God and sang exciting songs. Strangely, few people in the college thought of what they were singing; they just followed the words on the screens with their eyes and sang quietly, after all, it was a good way to impress the girls and look sophisticated. The college showed slides of students with sweat and shovel, and this was good.

The college wanted to help dirty people in a professional manner (of course), so they set up new ministry programs to meet with the changing needs of the world. "We must head for the cities!" they cried. Programs were drawn up and ideas were metamorphosed into dogma and academic credit was measured and instructional methods were developed and more trips to faraway places were planned.

The college got ready to make more t-shirts for the dump watchers, and everybody said "Amen!"

All the while the people in the white houses watched.

Always present at the college were the watchful eyes and the listening ears. For the college knew all about reality, and they were able to realize that there were dirty people hiding on campus, posing as students. The bad apples were sought out, for they were easy to spot.

Some bad apples just didn't dress right, others were missing some kind of point, there wasn't much time to be specific-enrollment was up and the more bad apples removed the better. They wouldn't be missed. They were dirty. They were in the way of the dream.

All the while the people in the white houses watched.

Of course, this dream was vague and rather undefined. It involved a streamlined form of Christianity that could be monitored by behavior and flaunted to the masses. The pretty people held the idea high, and it was catching on.

One day, a dirty student stopped going to classes and just began watching the college, in much the same way as the people in the white houses. His hair and his clothes spared him from tedious social expectations, and for this he was glad. He saw the idea, or something that looked like it had once been an idea. He realized that the idea was dying, or perhaps it was already dead, and there were just a few people moving its stiff limbs to give it the appearance of life.

He was sad because as he thought about the idea, it made good sense. The idea had been to help the people in the white houses. The idea had been to recognize the apple tree as divine and perfect, and to realize that all the apples were just as good and bad as each other. Unfortunately, a few of the bigger, prettier apples had started to resent the smaller spotted ones—for they were spoiling the group photo.

The dirty students realized that the programs and ideas and proposals and hand clapping were all techniques used by the stronger apples to change the focus of the lens, somehow to keep the small apples out of the public eye.

"Remember," spoke the biggest apple, "the only time you are to be seen with a dirty apple is when you are shoveling for him, you've seen were they end up, in the dump."

All the apples who followed him applauded and tied their Reeboks and snugged up their button-flys and practiced the secret handshake and squinted in an attractive, worldly way.

That night, the clean students piled off to the variety of programs created by the big apple, and some of them just went out for pizza. All in all, with teeth aglow and hugs waiting for those who deserved them, they drove right on by the street that led to the white houses and never looked up it.

The people in the white houses saw them go. The dirty students saw them go.

The moral of the story is: There's no such thing as a perfect apple. There is no ideal graduate. But there is, however, a time-honored, apathetic tradition that makes the college officials quickly remove or destroy all students who stray too far from the ideal.

I dare you to quit dump-gawking and hand-clapping, and treat the dirty people as if they were just the same as you.

The people in the white houses are watching.

Thanks, Steve. Thank you for being a living example. Think of all the joys, blessings, friendships, and love we miss because we are so muddled down in our Christian "works" that we miss the daily God-given-opportunities; opportunities to make a difference in someone's life, opportunities to make a difference in our own lives. To be sure, Steve, the people in the white houses are watching.

sh*t, cigarettes, and postmodernism
And why the Church can't respond to any of them!

Wait a minute! I thought you were an ordained minister. How dare you use profane words! What's wrong with you? Something needs to be done. We cannot allow pastors running around typing cuss words whenever they feel like it. What's next? Pastors in the town bars? Why don't we just have God himself turn water into wine for us? Wait! No, that was different.

It amazes me that so many churches in America have never figured out how to deal with people that drink, swear or smoke. Here's a thought. Let's pretend they are *real people* with *real problems* and love them. What if we accepted them "as is," and developed an honest relationship where we could share struggles and gently push each other to grow and discover faith. The big problem with that idea is not the unbelievers. They are looking for this type of relationship, longing for them. The problem is *us*. You see, in order to do that, we have to be real, honest, and accepting, and it seems there is just no place for that in the American Church.

I recently read a statistic that said over ninety percent of churches in North America are plateaued or declining in membership. It also seems that a major complaint of these churches is that they are plastic, totally fake. Most people outside of the church believe that the church is a place, not for them but only for those who are members of the church. We don't even need to debate where that message came from. The fact that it even *exists* should be enough to tell us something needs to change.

It seems the modern church has been on trial and the verdict is in: Guilty! We have been found guilty of creating a 'club' atmosphere where the pastor's main job is not to proclaim truth, but to cater to the members of the organization. We have been convicted on too many counts of members seeking to be entertained in the pew, rather than wanting to worship and engage God. We have been caught shunning the 'least of these' because cigarette butts are unsightly in the church parking lot. But worst of all, and the most condemning charge to date: We have preached one message and lived out quite another. This creates an unapproachable church that is cold, mechanical and quite unattractive. No wonder we have people leaving the church to save their faith!

Am I proposing that we water down the truth? Should pastors start swearing in their sermons? Should we just create a sinful free-for-all so everyone feels welcome? *No! No! No!* and let me hit you with another *No!* Of course not. Actually, that has been a big misunderstanding of postmodernism in the church. Anytime the subject is brought up, pastors and leaders think we are trying to throw everything out that the church as ever done and create this cultural anything-goes-chaos where we don't stand for anything. The other alternative is that postmodernism is just another program sent down the marketing pipe, aimed at selling books and filling seminars. Neither is true.

I will admit that the postmodern concept it difficult to get a mental handle on, so let me boil it down for you. 'Postmodern' is simply a title for the times in which we live. Our parents and grandparents grew up in the modern world. The world is changing. Computer technology, scientific advancements and discovery, cultural ideas, and many other factors are advancing the world in which we live. For a lack of another name, some have called it 'postmodern.' Basically, it means "the time after the modern world." The postmodern concept is troubling for many people for several reasons. One of the most significant reasons is that postmodernism is wrought with change, and change is always tough to swallow. Even if you are in favor of change, try getting a committee to agree on what that change should be. Change shakes people up. Change is messy.

Another problem exists because we are living in the transitional period of postmodernism. Imagine a continuum. On the far left is the modern world and on the far right is the postmodern world. Now place the people in your community on that line. They will be everywhere. It would be one thing if all people living on the West Coast were postmodern and everyone on the East Coast was modern. Or if everyone born before 1970 was modern and everyone after was postmodern. The problem is that neither is true. There are some sixty-year-old postmoderns, and some fifteen year old moderns and they are your neighbors. We all deal with new ideas, concepts and change quite differently. Add to all of this the fact that we don't even know what the emerging culture is going to look like, and you begin to understand the dilemma.

So why bother with the postmodern thing at all? There are many reasons to explore culture, change and post-modernity. But the best reason I can give you is that we simply don't have a choice. I stated earlier that the world is constantly changing and now changing at an accelerated pace. In today's world, we must adapt, or get left behind. And quite frankly, what do we have to lose? The church in America is in serious trouble. There are more churches closing than there are being opened. Most existing churches are not growing or are only growing laterally (people from one church simply move to another church.) How long can this continue before churches become an endangered species? To survive, we must become relevant to the culture we live in. That is what Jesus did.

Jesus came to earth as a man. He entered into and was part of the culture of his day. He did this without compromising his message, without sacrificing truth. Shouldn't we do the same? Postmodernism allows us, as the church, to engage the culture around us. For all of the problems that come with postmodernism, there are some great opportunities that make it more than worth the risk. As we enter into the cultural conversation, we will find our churches and the message of Christ becoming relevant. As we open ourselves up and let others see our struggles, and as we seek, we will build relationships with those who need Christ. The church will be transformed from that cold, mechanical "Elite Club" to an open, vibrant, organic community where believers welcome those searching and entertain their questions without condemnation or prejudice.

I do not claim to be an expert on drinking, swearing, smoking or postmodernism. But I am excited about what God will do when we give the control of the church back to Him. I have been a part of several different groups that have been studying this concept in the church. Every church, without fail, began with vision and passion and dependence on God. Over time, programs develop and order is established. And there is nothing wrong with this, unless these things become the idols of the church. When a church loves security and comfort more than fulfilling God's purpose, the passion and vision die. What if we begin to pray and search and ask tough questions? What would happen if we listened for the still, small voice of God and asked for vision and passion that was greater than ourselves? What if we allowed God to lead and move, even if it meant that we lost our sense of control and security? I can tell you what would happen, Chaos. But it would be God-ordained chaos, holy chaos with purpose and passion. What a ride! That is a church I want to be a part of.

"Now all has been heard; here is the conclusion of the matter: Fear God and keep his commandments, for this is the whole duty of man."

- Ecclesiastes 12:13 NIV

life in eight short chapters

chapter one: self

Strange title: Life in Eight Short Chapters. Strange indeed. Stranger still is the fact that it is not only *my* life, but *all* life. Can all life be condensed to a few pages of paper? I believe that life can be, but living cannot. Within this life, you must work out the living for yourself. There will be many people along the way that will guide and help you, but ultimately, it's your life. So let's get on with it.

We shall start at the beginning: the birth of self. For our purpose here, the person whose story I tell will be anonymous. Anonymous, because the searching in life could be applied to anyone.

What of this searching? Can this thing that man is groping for be labeled? Can it be identified? Hope? Wisdom? Meaning? Self? Understanding? Love? Life? It is all of these things, and it is none of them. It is man's destiny to search out his humanity. And that is my intent here. To search and to tell the story of a life. That brings me to the business at hand. To begin, we need a name. I will call him Christian. Why Christian? We'll leave you to sort that out. I simply offer this advice: don't get caught up in a name. Does the essence of a man lie within his name?

I will begin with the day Christian entered the world: his birth. I remember it as if it were yesterday. The freak April snow storm. The complete darkness outside. The only light was from the hospital. Man-made sodium light. I remember the mother's face, her eyes. Such love and pain in those eyes. I could reproduce every detail of that day. Every detail of the days that followed. But I will limit myself to the details that are important. And what was important to Christian in the early days was *Self*. Christian's world revolved around, well *Christian*.

Christian's early years were considered to be normal. He was sheltered and raised, loved and looked after. His was a false world. His every need was fulfilled with an immediate priority. He knew nothing of the world outside his shell. As his mother and father separated and then divorced, Christian was sheltered. Great efforts were made to keep his life normal. As a step-mother emerged, Christian was told it was normal. He learned to hide his emotions, and was told that too, was normal. Infants and children see their world through the lens of self. If self is okay, if self is normal, then life is okay and the world is normal. This is acceptable for children, but children grow and if left unchecked, self can eat you alive.

Chapter one begins and ends with self. Everything is about you. With time, self becomes a prison. A two-year-old who throws a tantrum because he doesn't get the candy he sees in the grocery store is simply a child that must learn that we don't always get what we want. But what if that lesson is never learned? The child becomes a man whose temper is out of control when he is disappointed. When that man's childish selfishness prevents him from a willingness to compromise or sacrifice in a marital relationship, frequently, it leads to divorce. Stop for a moment and think of sin. Can you think of one transgression that doesn't begin with selfishness? Difficult, if not impossible. Now we must move on; grow. And that is what Christian did.

chapter two: knowledge

I watched as Christian grew. Christian went through all the stages of life. The infant became a toddler. The toddler grew and entered nursery school. He explored the world around him with energetic fervor. Christian's world was expanding. New concepts were emerging. Christian was a sponge, absorbing everything. He was learning at incredible rates. But with knowledge came conflict. The desire for self had to be controlled. It was difficult to share and put others first. Christian wondered why? Why was it so difficult to stop being selfish?

As the years went by, school had begun to grow tedious and dull. "There has to be more to life," he thought. This quest for knowledge that used to be so exciting, so liberating, now seems to be a prison. Is this all there is? There has to be a better way to learn. Real life, it seemed, could teach Christian more than school ever could. Parents and teachers couldn't possibly know everything. Some things, you just have to discover on your own.

Christian's learning continued, as did his intense dissatisfaction. What he didn't realize, was that self had crept back into his life. He had controlled it in the external areas of his life, but now it was beginning to take over his mind. He wanted more. He wanted to be free to do whatever he pleased. Don't get me wrong, Christian's early life was not all trouble and conflict. Most of those years were carefree and fun. But looking back, a crisis was brewing.

Christian was becoming an adult. His world was opening up and expanding. And somewhere deep inside, something was stirring. The feeling was faint at first—vague. It took Christian by surprise. He never knew what hit him. It was a combination of self and growth and the love for fun that he had during those early years. It was almost as if they were conspiring against him. Amazing how simple life is in the beginning. Nothing to worry or stress over. All that exists is unconditional love and caring. There are no complexities of motives or hidden agendas. Words are taken at face value. Trust is simple, because it has never been broken. How do we lose the faith of a child? It seems to happen overnight, yet in reality, it is a gradual erosion over time. Can we ever go back? Only time would tell. As for Christian and our story, we must move on. That's the funny thing about living; life never stops until it's over.

chapter three: adventure

The stirring inside continued to grow, and although it was quite subconscious, it was the most powerful thing Christian had ever experienced. It began innocently enough. Christian loved to laugh. He loved to play, he loved fun. As Christian grew, so did his appetite for adventure. He discovered the excitement of sports, the freedom of driving a car, the adrenaline rush of breaking the rules, and the thrill of the opposite sex.

All of this was seen as normal, as well. Boys will be boys, and Christian was a good boy. Good by comparison, anyway. I guess it should be stated that he wasn't as bad as some other kids or at least, he didn't get caught as frequently. However you look at it, Christian was addicted to adventure. His world revolved around the next party, date, trip, event, or good time. This adventure-seeking lifestyle became all consuming during high school. It took up most of his time, and it consumed his thoughts. It controlled his actions and defined who he was. Growing up and breaking away from parents is an awkward stage. Discovering who you are is a never ending task. No wonder the temptation to have a little fun overcomes us at times. We all need a little break. But…How much is too much? Where do we draw the line? Christian had gained some wisdom and knowledge in his young life, enough to realize that adventure was not all there was to life. He saw that long time companion, selfishness at work in this too. But this time Christian was prepared. He was armed with logic and reason. He put it to the test. He used his wits to peer into the future.

What would a life that was built on a foundation of adventure look like? It wasn't hard to see. There were plenty of examples all around. Adventure takes many forms: love, lust, sex, material possessions, or simply playing at whatever you love. For Christian it was skiing. He loved skiing. He never had much use for alcohol or drugs, but he loved to conquer a snow covered mountain. There were other loves too. But all of them, if left in control, seemed to end in addiction and ruin. It became quite clear to Christian that pleasure could not be left in charge of his life. It certainly could be a big part of it, but he couldn't allow it to take control of him. Adventure *all* the time was yet another dead end street ending in a selfish, shallow life.

Knowledge was now becoming Christian's worst enemy. He has started out on a journey to discover the meaning of all this living. But he hadn't found one yet. Self only lead to selfishness. Knowledge just lead to more questions and became quite frustrating when there was no release, no pleasure and no adventure. But adventure wasn't the answer either. Christian lived several years trying to balance these pieces of life, yet somehow, he knew there had to be more. The *more* came out of necessity. Adventure was expensive and Christian was about to graduate from high school. His pursuit of knowledge would now cost money, as well. Christian did the only thing he could do; he got a job.

chapter four: work

Work is where it's at! That was the first thought Christian had as he headed into the bank and cashed his first paycheck. "I'm rich," he screamed within the confines of his mind. "Time for some fun!" Freeze! Do you see it there? Almost unnoticeable. Appears logical. Christian worked hard for two entire weeks, and now it was payday, at long last! Time to play. What could be more natural than spending what you have earned? What could be more satisfying? What could be more addicting? Look again, look closer. *I have some cash. Time for some fun.* Within those two statements, the stage was set for a lifelong addiction. This is the stuff workaholics are made of.

It is the marriage of the selfish pursuit of pleasure to the intoxicating power of money. And what brought this couple together? Work. Work introduced these two strangers and suggested they go out. Careers are interesting animals. It is a love/hate relationship. Careers are a necessity, and can be extremely satisfying. On the other hand, they can become another prison in the routine life of corporate America. We want more, more, more so we work harder, longer, and faster. It is the perpetual "if only" that keeps America alive. If only I had $20,000 dollars, I would be out of debt…If only I had a bigger house, a better car…If only I had a new wardrobe…If only I could take that vacation…If only I could afford a new television…If only I could buy that boat, and then that bigger boat and then that bigger better boat. Consumerism, workaholic-syndrome, and the pursuit of pleasure. We work more to get more, only to discover we have no time to enjoy anything.

Christian saw himself, but it really wasn't *him*. He was older. Forget older, he was old. But he was powerful. He had worked his entire life. He started with nothing and worked his way to the top of the corporate ladder. He was respected. He had everything. But then he looked closer. He was wrinkled, gray, he was tired, he was cynical. He had lost his family to his career. He had no true friends, only business contacts. His power and his wealth were about to be left behind, because Christian had developed cancer, and all of his money and power and influence couldn't buy him one more minute of life. Even if someone cured cancer, in the end death always came out on top. It's a game you just can't cheat. Christian realized that he had nothing of lasting value. He thought he left pleasure behind, only to find that his work had become his pleasure, his life. He told himself in the beginning that he was doing it for his family, and that he wasn't selfish. When the family abandoned him, the voice just stopped talking altogether. Where had he gone wrong? It couldn't be to late…all he heard was a buzzing.

The buzzing woke Christian up. It was his alarm clock. He was young again. It was his first day of his first job. As he dug himself out from under the warmth of his blankets, he paused.

This is either the first or the last day of the rest of my life, he thought to himself.

chapter five: relationships

The job was going well. Training was just about over and Christian actually enjoyed the work. He loved the money although he wished it was more, but something else surprised him. He was forming friendships at his job. Sure, he'd always had friends. But something was different this time. These friends seemed closer, one in particular. It wasn't because of the minimum wage job, so what was the difference? Christian wasn't the most popular kid in his class, but he had always made it a priority to have good friends, lifelong friends. So what was changing? As Christian thought about it, he realized it wasn't just the people at work. It was everyone. His old friendships seemed different too. Christian had discovered the power of relationships in life. Up until now, friendship had been based on shared experience and social proximity. Shared space, and shared interests, equaled instant friends. But now Christian was experiencing different viewpoints, different interest and deeper friendships. As he grew in knowledge, age, and experience, he decided it was time to test his social wings. He discovered this was another way to learn, it was a new form of pleasure. As a child, he had cared about self and self alone. Christian now found himself caring about others.

One of those "others" found her way to the top of the relationship pyramid. Christian was in love. Love was amazing, albeit a little hard to define. But Christian was too in love to worry or to even see that. His world was upside down. He was putting others first and finding pleasure in it. He was spending money and working for others.

Christian was happy and satisfied with this, (or at least distracted and naïve, depending on how you look at it.) Whichever, it didn't matter. Christian finally felt like life had both meaning and purpose. And it did, for a while. But with pleasure there is always pain; and with joy, sorrow. Days filled with companionship and love gave way to nights of loneliness and an unquenchable, empty feeling. What began so well, ended quite horribly. Christian discovered that some relationships weren't meant to last. He discovered a new kind of hurt. It was the pain of giving yourself away to someone else, only to be rejected. Christian withdrew, filling his head with sad love songs on the radio. He wallowed in self-pity and found he had too much spare time to think depressing thoughts. He didn't know it yet, but this would lead him to one of his greatest discoveries of all.

chapter six: faith

The discovery didn't just happen. It appeared out of nowhere but in reality had been slowly forming inside Christian since childhood. Looking back, the first glimpse came one warm summer afternoon. It was one of those carefree childhood days. Christian had been swimming and afterward he stretched out in the sun, enjoying the warmth. It was there that he first caught a glimpse of it. He saw the vast expanse of the sky. It consumed everything. There was no end in sight. Just deep blue everywhere. It overpowered Christian's finite mind. It made him think of God, the God he had heard about in Sunday School. But who was that God? Christian knew only of a ritualistic and ceremonial God that existed within the confines of a church that he was forced to attend. Who was this new God that Christian saw in the sky?

There were other faith sightings as Christian grew up, as well. He just didn't recognize them. As the radio played another love song, the pieces all fit together in Christian's mind. He had been searching for meaning in this life without thinking about the next. What happens when you die? Why am I here? What's the meaning of life? Maybe the joy he had discovered in relationships was meant to teach him about an even greater relationship. Maybe in this life, people let you down, but if there is a next life, would it be perfect?

The questions kept coming and coming and Christian knew he didn't have all the answers. He realized discovering this was something far more valuable. For the first time in his life, Christian felt like there was more to life than knowledge. There was faith. Faith to hang on for something better, faith that this life is not the end, and faith that everything was not in vain. He had a sense that there was a God and He was the one in control. Faith. There is true pleasure in faith. There is wisdom in faith. Self can be given away in faith, never to be rejected. This was a brand new relationship. A brand new way of living and Christian couldn't wait to start.

chapter seven: servanthood

Christian realized, for the first time, what he had been looking for all this time. Only, he had been looking in all the wrong places. It took the pain of a broken relationship for him to realize that he was selfish and that what he was looking for was wholeness. That unconditional love he felt as a child was still his. He didn't deserve it, and he couldn't earn it by working harder or longer. It was free as only grace can be. Free for the asking. All those years he dared not to ask. They seemed such a waste.

He had so much to learn. He had to make up for so much lost time. Christian didn't want to live with any regrets. As he slept, he had another dream. He was old again and in this life, time was running out. But in *this* dream, it was okay. He wasn't cynical; he wasn't lonely. This time he looked back on life and smiled. He hoped others knew why he was smiling.

That was it. Christian stopped daydreaming. All those years were not wasted. Not unless he didn't use them now. Those years contained his story and others need to hear it. If selfishness was not the answer, maybe servanthood was. Christian would give himself away to others. Even if the others rejected him, he knew that it would be okay. There was a joy in serving that has nothing to do with getting something back. In fact, a true servant expects nothing in return. The joy is in the faith that you are living life for the one that gave you life.

    Christian stopped. He thought. He smiled. He had just discovered the key to life.

chapter eight: wholeness

Christian had the key but not all of the answers. But he didn't need them. He was on the right path. Christian looked back over his relatively young life and marveled. He marveled at how far he had come and how he had gotten there. He was amazed at how far he still had to go and wondered how on earth he would make it. His mother adjusted the tassel on his cap and looked at the gown. "I can't believe my baby is graduating from high school," she said. *You have no idea,* thought Christian. He was somewhat fearful as he faced the future, but there was a certain steadiness, too.

Christian knew this road would lead to wholeness. It would be the road that would take him home. He wanted answers about what it meant to be fully human. He faced the future with questions. All this time and he still didn't know.

Not knowing…what a great gift. It takes all the pressure off. Not knowing makes every day an adventure; every moment sacred. It forces us to discover faith and relationships. It gives us a passion for knowledge. Work and money are worthy and honorable pursuits. Pleasure is great in moderation. Balance is the dance of life and faith is the music. Explore, discover, wonder, enjoy. After all, it's only life.

Life in Eight Short Chapters, sure. Living life, that takes every moment you have. Better get to it!

Yesterday is but a memory; the future - distant, cold, and uncertain. All we have is the moment. How many moments will be wasted on the past and future before we realize there is only today?

i could die tomorrow

I could die tomorrow. Have I lived today? The writer of Ecclesiastes assures all of mankind that "There is a time for everything, and a season for every activity under heaven…" Time for laughing and crying; mourning and dancing; there is a time to be born and a time to die. All men are born and all men die. It is what is done in between, what is done in the now that matters.

And that is what perplexes me. My "nows" are not so great. Oh, the list of excuses goes on and on, and being the educated type, I can make them sound so good. The outside observer would hardly recognize them at all. If I don't want to work, I simply say I need to spend time with my family. I take on the appearance of a loyal, devoted family man. If my family begins to get on my last nerve, I, the famous chameleon, become the dedicated office man. But to see the worst case scenario, one has to peek into the dark recesses of my mind and look at the justification for the evil conjured up there. The malice, envy, desire, and self-centeredness take over. There are no excuses given, because the public must never see that side. The public sees only the skin. The war that rages beneath, rages in the mind alone. But the casualty count spreads to all that know me…only…they never know what hit them. They think, "Why is he acting that way?" Or, "Man is he moody." We all see the results and never question the place of their origin. Society has taught us how to play that game well. Because if I call you into question, I must be prepared to be transparent and show myself, as well. But we can't let that happen at any cost, on any level, can we? Oh, occasionally the educated ones will give the appearance of being transparent. It is important to them that we see just how deep and well rounded they are. Yet this too is a carefully constructed facade; simply another layer. The irony is that we fight to be free by hiding. And true freedom comes in honesty. Honestly, I fear that if I peel back all the layers, there will be no substance; no core. Am I living an onion-skinned life? I have all the right skins that I put on at all the right times, and I am very good at it. But strip it all away and throw the layers in the garbage. Was there anything underneath it all? I could die tomorrow.

How would I be remembered? What great things have I done? I don't mean "great" as in political battles fought or world peace. I am thinking more of inner peace and personal battles overcome. The very struggles each of us have everyday are the ones we hide and fight alone. Tomorrow I die. Does anyone know me today? Do they see me, the real me? Do they know they are truly, unconditionally loved? Have I learned to love that way and accept it from others? Some men live for years and never really live, while others live an entire life in a day. I look at past photographs of those who have gone before me. No one famous, just ordinary people like me: A high school yearbook from 1923, a church photo from 1894. They were forgotten. Did they wait too long to live? Did they have a today worth dying for? What were their dreams? Time passes, standards change, but through it all living remains the same. The questions are universal: Why am I here? Where am I going? What does it all mean? I could die tomorrow.

And if today is my last day on earth, am I satisfied? Am I ready to go? Are we ever really ready? What does death hold? What about those I leave behind? Did I spend too much time covering up the dirty little secrets of the past and working hard to do better next time, that those I love today never saw me? Did I have a real purpose? I am pretty sure the answer to that question does not lie in how much money I made, or in any other layer of myself that I have presented to the world. Success is not judged by man's standards on the other side. The answer is found only in the essence, the core, the heart. And the essence can never be fully seen by the human eye. Yet I know there is a rhythm and reason to my today. There has to be. Without it everything is meaningless. I could die tomorrow.

Maybe that is the answer. Maybe the answers lie not in the finding but in the searching. There has to be some substance in every question that remains, even if we never find an answer. Maybe the essence of who we are is not to be tangibly grasped but rather, something to be experienced. If I live today searching for meaning instead of constructing false faces and whitewashing my appearance, then perhaps the yesterdays and tomorrows wouldn't matter so much. Maybe life is full of paradox and contradiction. Maybe the only way I can truly live today is to give today away. If at the heart of every evil and sin is self-centeredness, maybe I should put the *self* to death. Not a physical death, mind you, but a laying of selfishness to rest. The simplicity of a life lived for others could unlock the secrets of the universe. Could it be that I am right here, right now for no other purpose than to love those around me? God never said I would see God in me. He said I would see Him in others and as I serve others, they would see Him in me. Could it be that simple? Is that why the old man on his death bed can smile? Is that the difference between 'living' and 'just being alive'? I could die tomorrow.

So is living today really that easy? Just give yourself away, love others, be content, and never stop searching? Is that the secret of success? If that really *is* the answer, it will never be easy. Since our infancy, too often and in too many ways, we have been taught just the opposite. "The Ways of the World are Wise." In a sublime manner, we have learned the importance of phrases like, "Be a man," "Support your family," "Never show weakness, after all you have to be the rock."

Society has elevated evil to an art form. We are enticed and dizzied until we exchange the *best* stuff for the *good* stuff; the truth for a well-crafted, fabulous sounding lie. And we buy into the lie at the expense of our family and friends. We soak up the world-view that says "Live the past, chase the future and miss today." Unfortunately, we don't hear the "and miss today" part. Today is all I really have. I could die tomorrow.

Life and Death; Hope and Fear; Love and Hate - a thin line separates us in every way. The line is blurred, the path is muddy and the way is easily lost. Is the beginning found at the finish line? Nothing is as it seems. Perspectives change, as life is lived.

We live waiting for tomorrow. What if it never comes?

shoulda, coulda, woulda

"Did you ever have a dream?" he asked.

"Sure," I said as I paused the DVD player. "Don't we all," I replied as I went to grab the chips and another soda.

"What was it?"

"What?" I called from the kitchen.

"What was it? Your dream, I mean."

I rounded the corner and sat back down in the recliner. "I don't know…it was more than this, that's for sure."

"What happened?"

"What do you mean what happened?" I asked, getting a little annoyed and wanting to resume the movie.

"To your dream, what happened?"

"Life happened," I said defeated. "You know, I have a wife and a mortgage, two car payments, a job I don't like…life."

"Is that enough? Don't you want more?"

"Sure…someday I guess."

"Ask yourself this," he said, "what would you do if you didn't have a wife and a mortgage, the car payment and commitments?"

As I pondered that, he got up and said he had to go.

He stopped at the door and turned. "One more thing, once you think of what it is, ask yourself why you are letting a mortgage stop you."

He was gone, and I grabbed the remote and pushed play.

Whole

adj.

1. Containing all components; complete.
2. Not divided or disjoined; in one unit.
3. Constituting the full amount, extent, or duration.
4. a. Not wounded, injured, or impaired; sound or unhurt.
   b. Having been restored; healed.

Half

adj.
Partial or incomplete

adv.
Not completely or sufficiently; partly

wholly half

I want to be whole! It is the cry of my heart. To be complete, unified, balanced. I want to have one purpose, one vision, and one reason, a *whole* reason. It is the reason I keep going, keep searching, and keep struggling. It is the desire that picks me up when I fall; time after time. I press onward for no other reason. I try and try again so that one day I may reach the dream.

I want to be whole! It is the cry of my heart. Free of contradiction; freed from fear and lies, no longer wavering. True to myself and my beliefs; able to look myself in the mirror and like what I see. I need to be whole for the people around me; my family and friends. I want to be strong for myself and for others.

I want to be whole! It is the cry of my heart. Not to be perfect. I don't think perfection would indicate wholeness. Not to be lifeless; void of emotion. On the contrary, I want to be wholly passionate; filled with godly desire. I want to live a great adventure. Chase my dreams, throw caution to the wind. Wholly live, wholly love.

I want to be whole! It is the cry of my heart. But I am not. I am half. Half-hearted; half-committed; half-way; half dead. I am an unbalanced, incomplete man. I know what I want. I hear the cry and yet, I fall short. I come up wanting. I am needy, I am fickle, I am wandering. Some days, it seems so easy; just all falls into place. Other days, I am doomed from the time I get out of bed. I want to be whole.

But I am not. Not even close; not by a long shot. I want to be disciplined in body, mind and spirit. I want to lose fifteen pounds. I want to read more. I want to learn. I want to grow. I want to be farther today than I was yesterday. I want to love more and complain less. I want to be a better father. I want to be a better husband. I want to be more awake. I wish I wanted it all enough to do something about it.

But I don't. There are days I try so hard and then the very next day, I just don't care—at all. I see my dreams. I have goals, and yet here I sit; half—not whole. Close, but not close enough. Strong, in a weak sort of way. I can't do it. At least not all of it, not today.

I want to be whole! It is the cry of my heart. And I will hold on to that cry. I will cling to that desire. I will not give up. It will not happen overnight, but it will happen; slowly. At times, unnoticeably, but it will happen. I will fall. I will mess up. It will be two steps forward and three steps back at times. That is life. It is not an excuse, and it will not make me quit, ever; at least not for very long.

I can't do it alone. So I won't. I will share my troubles with those I love; those I trust. I will risk because I believe they have problems, too. I believe they want to be whole. I believe we are in this together: a community. I believe that a community of seekers, open, honest, seekers will be greater than the sum of its members. I believe math is wrong. Wholeness does not come from addition, it comes from subtraction. I need to subtract pride from the equation. I need to subtract self: self-sufficiency and selfishness. I need to give, to pour myself into others. As I look back on my life, that is when I am most whole; most complete. It's when I give and serve and love.

I want to be whole! I will start right now, in simple ways; in small choices. I will rise above. I can. I will. I must.

I want to be whole!
It is the cry of my heart.

i'm not right

But thank God, neither are you.

Fascinating. It amazes me how you can read the title of this chapter, "I'm not right," and wholeheartedly agree, almost to the point of happiness. (Wipe that smile off your face.) And yet, the next line causes anger and…dare I say a little fear? Fear that it might be true. Don't be offended. It is true, you know. We aren't right. Not about everything. We can't be. Think about it. Let it sink in. Say it out loud as an acknowledgement first. Now say it again as a confession, "I am not right." Louder now as a proclamation: *I am not right!*

Healing begins here. This is the stuff that brings walls down. May it spread from you to your friends and family. May it be heard in the church and in the community. It creates a holy ground. It is common ground on which we can all stand and share. It is a place to start. Meditate on the implications. If I am not right, I might be wrong. I might need to learn; to grow. I might want to listen more and talk less. I might want to search for understanding.

I am not right, not all the time. My way is not best, not every time. If I can admit that and live out that premise and if you can as well, then I believe we have done more for peace and harmony than you can possibly imagine. It could quite possibly be the dawn of a new day. It would be a major step toward ending racism and hate crimes. I believe this common ground is a seed which will grow into a world we have never seen. It is what we were created for. It is why we are here. It is how religion becomes spiritual and how the spiritual is expressed. Close your eyes and imagine.

See the future; a future without the pressure of always being right. A future without segregation. A future understood through an open mind. A future where one way is not the only way. A future of people joining hands instead of clenching fists. It could happen, couldn't it?

I want to believe that it could. I need to believe that it could. Not to the point of utopia. I don't think we will see perfection on this side of life. There will still be problems, but think of the possibilities. Can you? Will you? Follow it through in your lifetime, however long it is. What does it look like if you are right and I am wrong? Wasted time, wasted energy, wasted relationships. Now shift. Really shift. What does it look like with just a little understanding? Reach out and take my hand. I'm drowning, not waving, you know. There is a place, a starting place, a common place. If you will meet me there; think of what might happen, in my life, in yours.

I'm not right. I'm willing to say it. I thank God for it. Now it's up to you. Remember, these are just my rants. Ramblings left rattling around in my head. Take from them what you will. You don't have to listen to me. I'm dead, remember? It's too late for me. But if you will hear, I will sum up my life with three thoughts:

You don't have to buy the lie.

You don't have to settle.

You really don't have to eat that potato salad.

Hey, what are you still doing here? The book is over. It's done: finished. You're out of excuses. Drop the book and go live. Live life while there's still life to live.